NORTHERN ITALY TRAVEL GUIDE 2025

Discover Scenic Itineraries, Hidden Gems, Authentic Local Experiences, and Must-See Destinations from Milan to Venice, Lake Como, and the Dolomites

Albert N. Allred

Copyright © 2024 (Albert N. Allred)

All rights reserved. No part of this book may be reproduced or transmitted in any form or by any means, electronic or mechanical, including photocopying, recording or by any information storage and retrieval system, without written permission from the author, except for the inclusion of brief quotations embodied in critical reviews and certain other non commercial uses permitted by copyright law.

Disclaimer

Welcome to Your **Northern Italy Travel Guide 2025**! Get ready to experience the best of Northern Italy with this comprehensive guide, packed with insider tips and must-see spots. From the romantic canals of Venice and the artistic treasures of Florence to the scenic beauty of Lake Como and the vibrant streets of Milan, we'll help you uncover the magic of this stunning region.

Keep in mind that Northern Italy's charm and lively spirit mean that prices, hours, and schedules can sometimes change. To ensure a smooth journey, double-check details with your hotels, tour operators, and attractions before you go.

Think of this guide as your trusted companion, ready to lead you through unforgettable adventures. With a little planning, your trip to Northern Italy will be everything you've dreamed of and more.

Buon viaggio!

Table of Contents

Introduction 7

Chapter 1: Welcome to Northern Italy 10

    A. A Brief History of Northern Italy.. 10

    B. Why Visit Northern Italy in 2025? 13

    C. Geography and Climate............. 15

Chapter 2: Planning Your Trip........... 18

    A. Getting to Northern Italy: Best Airports................................. 18

    B. Transportation in the Northern Italy......................................22

    C. When to Visit................................24

    D. Visa and Entry Requirements....27

    E. Currency, Costs, and Budget Tips 30

    F. Travel Insurance and Safety Tips.. 34

    G. Packing Essentials...................... 38

Chapter 3 Top Destinations in

Northern Italy............................ 43
   A. Venice................................43
   B. Milan................................ 47
   C. Florence........................... 51
   D. Lake Como.......................54
   E. Cinque Terre....................59
   F. Turin................................. 63
   G. Verona............................. 66
   H. Bologna............................70

Chapter 4: Hidden Gems and Off-the-Beaten-Path Destinations...75
   A. Exploring the Quiet Villages of the Dolomites...........................75
   B. Discovering the Prosecco Hills. 78
   C. The Charming Lakeside Town of Bellagio................................ 82
   D. The Unseen Beauty of Friuli Venezia Giulia........................ 86
   E. Modena.............................91
   F. Parma...............................95

Chapter 5: Itinerary Planning......... 100
   A. 7-Day Highlights Itinerary....... 100
   B. 10-Day Comprehensive Itinerary..

103

C. 14-Day In-Depth Itinerary........107

Chapter 6: Cultural Experiences......111

A. Must-Visit Museums and Art Galleries... 111

B. Historic Sites and Architectural Wonders..113

C. Local Festivals and Events You Can't Miss..116

Chapter 7: The Culinary Delights of Northern Italy... 121

A. Traditional Dishes You Must Try.. 121

B. Best Restaurants You Should Consider... 125

C. Wine Regions and Tasting Tours.. 127

Chapter 8: Outdoor Activities and Adventures...132

A. Hiking in the Italian Alps and Dolomites...132

B. Lake Activities: Sailing, Kayaking, and Swimming..............................136

C. Winter Sports..................139
D. Biking Through Scenic Countryside Trails..........................143

Chapter 9: Shopping in Northern Italy..................................148

A. Luxury Shopping in Milan........ 148

B. Local Markets and Artisan Shops. 153

C. What to Buy.......................... 158

Chapter 10: Accommodation Guide...... 164

A. Top Hotels, Boutique Stays, and Budget Options...............................164

B. Eco-Friendly and Unique Accommodation Choices.............. 168

Chapter 11: Practical Information...173

A. Emergency Contacts and Safety Tips for Travelers............................173

B. Health and Wellness................... 177

C. Language Tips and Useful Italian Phrases...181

Conclusion.. 186

Bonus: Authentic Northern Italian

Recipes.. 188

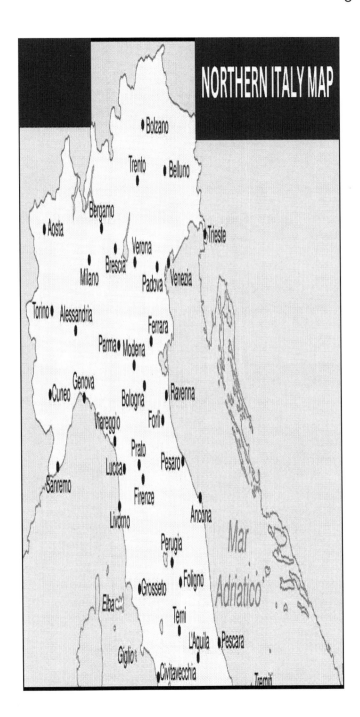

Introduction

Ciao, amici!

So, you're dreaming of Northern Italy, huh? Fantastico! I've been lucky enough to wander through this incredible region countless times, and let me tell you, it's like stepping into a real-life postcard. Every time I visit, I discover something new and fall even more in love with its charming towns, breathtaking landscapes, and delicious food (oh, the food!).

My latest trip in 2024 was pure magic. It was like Northern Italy opened its arms and welcomed me like an old friend, sharing its secrets and showing me just how special it truly is.

One of my favorite memories? Stumbling upon a tiny trattoria tucked away in a quiet alley in Florence. Picture this: red-checked tablecloths, the aroma of freshly baked bread and simmering sauces, and the sound of laughter and lively conversation. I savored the most incredible pasta dish, made with love by a nonna (grandmother) who's been perfecting her recipe for generations. It was a true taste of Italy! (And guess what? You can find it too - I'll tell you exactly where!).

Another unforgettable experience was hiking in the Dolomites. I woke up early, laced up my boots, and set off on a trail that wound through meadows filled with wildflowers, past crystal-clear lakes, and up to a breathtaking viewpoint. The air was crisp and clean, the views were simply stunning, and I felt like I was on top of the world.

Of course, no trip to Northern Italy is complete without a gondola ride in Venice. Imagine gliding along the canals in a beautiful gondola, the gentle rocking motion lulling you into a state of pure bliss. You'll pass under ancient bridges, admire grand palazzos, and soak up the unique charm of this magical city.

But Northern Italy is more than just beautiful scenery and delicious food. It's the people I met along the way that made my trip truly special. I chatted with a passionate gondolier in Venice who shared his family's history with the city. I learned how to make fresh pasta from scratch with a local chef in Bologna. And in a small village in Tuscany, I shared a glass of wine with a family who welcomed me like one of their own.

These are the kinds of moments that make Northern Italy so unforgettable. It's not just about seeing amazing things; it's about the experiences you have and the connections you make.

So, what are you waiting for? Grab this guide, start planning your adventure, and get ready to fall in love with Northern Italy! Who knows, maybe we'll bump into each other in a piazza, enjoying a gelato under the Italian sun!

Chapter 1: Welcome to Northern Italy

A. A Brief History of Northern Italy

I can tell you're already excited about your trip to Northern Italy, and trust me, you should be! But before we jump into all the fun things to see and do, let me share a bit of history. Don't worry—I'll keep it simple and easy, like chatting with a friend over coffee.

Picture Northern Italy thousands of years ago, way before any of the cities we know today existed. The first people here were living in small tribes, using the rivers and mountains to fish, hunt, and gather. You can still find ancient carvings in the Alps that tell us these early settlers were already creating art and building small communities.

Then came the Etruscans, around 2,000 years before Christ. These folks were amazing traders and artists. They set up small towns where places like Bologna and Florence now stand. They loved making things from metal and pottery, and they started traditions that influenced the entire region. Pretty soon, though, they had company.

By about 400 BC, the Celtic tribes moved in, bringing their own culture and way of life. They loved the rugged hills and valleys, setting up little villages and living off the land. But it wasn't long before the mighty Roman Empire showed up, ready to take control.

The Romans completely transformed Northern Italy. They built incredible roads, amphitheaters, and temples. You can still visit some of these ancient sites today, like the arena in Verona, where they used to host big shows and events. Milan even became one of the main capitals of the Roman Empire, filled with busy markets and grand buildings.

After the Roman Empire fell, things got a bit chaotic. Different groups like the Visigoths and the Lombards swept through the area, each leaving their mark. The Lombards, especially, became a big part of the region's history, and that's why we still have a region called Lombardy today. They built castles and settled in the fertile plains, mixing their traditions with what the Romans left behind.

Next came the Middle Ages, and Northern Italy became a land of powerful city-states. Imagine cities like Venice, Florence, and Genoa acting like mini-countries, each with its own rulers, armies, and incredible wealth. Venice was a superstar of the sea, trading goods from Asia and Africa. Florence, on the other hand, was all about art and creativity, sparking the Renaissance—a time when famous artists like Leonardo da Vinci and Michelangelo created their masterpieces.

In the 1800s, everything changed again. Northern Italy was caught up in wars and revolutions, especially during the time of Napoleon. It was a rough time, but it led to something incredible: the unification of Italy. By 1861, Italy became one country, thanks to leaders like Garibaldi who fought hard for independence.

Then came the 20th century, and Northern Italy became a powerhouse of industry and fashion. Milan led the way, becoming the fashion capital we know today. Companies in cities like Turin made fast cars (think Ferrari and Fiat!), while Milan became famous for its stylish clothes. But life wasn't all easy—the World Wars hit Northern Italy hard, with battles fought in the mountains and cities bombed. Still, the people rebuilt their homes and cities, showing the kind of spirit and resilience that defines this region.

Today, Northern Italy is a magical mix of old and new. One minute, you're walking through ancient

Roman ruins, and the next, you're shopping at a trendy boutique or sipping a cappuccino in a modern café. Everywhere you go, you'll feel the history all around you, from the cobblestone streets of Florence to the grand canals of Venice.

B. Why Visit Northern Italy in 2025?

If you're thinking about visiting Northern Italy in 2025, you've made a fantastic choice! This year is shaping up to be an exciting time, and there's so much to experience. From incredible events and delicious food to stunning scenery and local charm, Northern Italy is ready to welcome you with open arms. Let's dive into why 2025 is the perfect year to go.

1. Big Events and Festivals

Get ready for an unforgettable experience! The Venice Biennale is celebrating its 125th anniversary in 2025, making it a must-see for art lovers. You'll find incredible exhibitions from artists around the world, set against the romantic backdrop of Venice's canals. Then there's Milan Fashion Week, where the city transforms into a hub of style and glamour. Whether you're a fashion fan or just curious, the buzz in Milan during this week is electric, and the city feels more alive than ever.

2. Easy Travel and Day Trips

Traveling around Northern Italy has never been easier. With upgraded high-speed trains, you can hop from Milan to Lake Como in under 40 minutes. Imagine starting your day shopping in Milan and ending it with a peaceful boat ride on the lake. Plus, direct trains now connect you to places like the Dolomites, perfect for hiking or skiing. It's a great year for exploring beyond the major cities and discovering hidden gems.

3. A Focus on Sustainable Tourism

If you care about eco-friendly travel, you'll love what Northern Italy is doing in 2025. Many hotels and restaurants are focusing on sustainability, offering organic, farm-to-table dining and eco-certified accommodations. You can visit a biodynamic vineyard in Piedmont or take a guided hike through the preserved paths of the Dolomites, all while helping to protect the beautiful landscapes.

4. Food and Wine Experiences

2025 is a fantastic year for foodies. Northern Italy's culinary scene is booming, with chefs blending traditional recipes with new, creative ideas. From fresh truffle dishes in Alba to the famous risotto in Milan, every meal is a chance to taste the heart of the region. Don't miss the local wines, like the crisp whites of the Veneto and the bold reds of Barolo. Each sip is a taste of the landscape.

5. Unique Local Adventures

Looking for something special? Join a cooking class in Bologna to make fresh pasta or take a sunset cruise on Lake Garda. Explore small village festivals in the Alps, where you can enjoy local music, dance, and taste homemade cheese. It's a great way to meet friendly locals and experience the true spirit of Northern Italy.

C. Geography and Climate

Let's take a closer look at what makes Northern Italy's geography and climate so unique.

1. The Majestic Alps and Dolomites

Let's start with the Alps, which form the northern border of Italy. These snow-capped giants are a paradise for outdoor lovers, offering some of the best hiking and skiing in Europe. The Dolomites, a part of the Alps known for their dramatic, jagged peaks, are particularly stunning. If you love adventure, this is the place to be, with activities like rock climbing, mountain biking, and scenic drives that show off breathtaking views around every corner.

2. The Tranquil Lakes

Northern Italy is also famous for its beautiful lakes. Lake Como, Lake Garda, and Lake

Maggiore are the stars here, each with its own personality. Lake Como feels like a glamorous postcard, with charming villages and elegant villas dotting its shores. Lake Garda, the largest, is great for families and water sports, while Lake Maggiore offers a peaceful escape with stunning islands and gardens to explore. The lakes bring a sense of calm and are perfect for relaxing boat rides, picnics, or simply enjoying the view.

3. The Fertile Po Valley

Stretching across the heart of Northern Italy is the Po Valley, a flat, fertile plain that's crucial for the region's agriculture. This is where you'll find endless fields of rice, corn, and vineyards. It's the land of risotto and wine, and it's known for its delicious produce, from fresh tomatoes to sweet peaches. The Po River, Italy's longest river, winds its way through this valley, supporting the farmlands and giving life to the countryside.

4. The Charming Coastline

To the east, the region meets the sea along the Adriatic Coast, home to the famous city of Venice. The coastline here is dotted with beautiful beaches and charming seaside towns. It's a great spot for sunbathing, swimming, and enjoying fresh seafood right by the water.

5. The Climate

Because the geography of Northern Italy is so varied, the climate can be quite different depending on where you are. In the mountains, expect chilly winters with lots of snow—a skier's dream! Summers in the Alps are mild and perfect for hiking, with cool breezes and clear skies. Down in the Po Valley, the climate is more temperate, with hot summers and cool, foggy winters.

By the lakes, the climate is generally mild, making it a favorite spot year-round. You'll find warm, sunny summers perfect for swimming, and the winters are cool but not too harsh. Along the coast, you'll enjoy a typical Mediterranean climate, with warm, sunny days and mild, breezy nights—a perfect combination for beach vacations.

Chapter 2: Planning Your Trip

A. Getting to Northern Italy: Best Airports

Here's a detailed guide to the major airports in the region, including their locations, transportation options, and associated costs.

1. Milan Malpensa Airport (MXP)

- **Location:** Approximately 49 kilometers (30 miles) northwest of Milan, in the Lombardy region.

- **Overview:** As Northern Italy's largest airport, Malpensa serves as a major international hub, connecting travelers to destinations worldwide. It's particularly convenient for those visiting Milan, Lake Como, or the Italian Alps.

Transportation to/from the Airport:
- **Train:** The Malpensa Express connects the airport to Milan's city center in about 50 minutes. Tickets cost €13 for a one-way journey.
- **Bus:** Several bus services operate between the airport and key locations in Milan. Tickets are typically priced at €10 for a one-way trip.
- **Taxi:** Available outside the terminals; a ride to central Milan has a fixed fare of €95.

2. Venice Marco Polo Airport (VCE)

SCAN THE QR CODE

1. Open your device camera app.
2. Position the QR code in the camera frame.
3. Hold your phone steady.
4. Wait for the code to be recognized.
5. Once recognized, tap on the notification or follow the prompt to access the content or action associated with the Qr code

- **Location:** Approximately 13 kilometers (8 miles) north of Venice, in the Veneto region.

- **Overview:** Named after the famous explorer, this airport is the primary gateway to Venice and its surrounding areas. It's ideal for travelers planning to explore the Venetian canals, historic sites, and nearby islands.

Transportation to/from the Airport:
- **Water Bus (Alilaguna):** Offers a scenic route directly to Venice's main areas. Tickets cost €15 for a one-way trip.
- **Bus:** ACTV and ATVO buses connect the airport to Piazzale Roma in Venice. The ATVO express bus service costs €8 for a one-way ticket or €15 for a return ticket.
- **Taxi:** Land taxis are available; water taxis provide a direct but pricier option to Venice's canals, with fares starting around €100.

3. Bologna Guglielmo Marconi Airport (BLQ)

SCAN THE QR CODE

1. Open your device camera app.
2. Position the QR code in the camera frame.
3. Hold your phone steady.
4. Wait for the code to be recognized.
5. Once recognized, tap on the notification or follow the prompt to access the content or action associated with the Qr code

- **Location:** Approximately 10 kilometers (6 miles) northwest of Bologna's city center, in the Emilia-Romagna region.

- **Overview:** Serving as a key hub in Northern Italy, this airport is perfect for travelers heading to Bologna, Florence, and other central Italian cities.

Transportation to/from the Airport:
- **Marconi Express:** A monorail connecting the airport to Bologna Centrale railway station in 7 minutes. Tickets cost €9.20 for a one-way journey.
- **Bus:** Aerobus services link the airport to the city center, with tickets priced at €6.
- **Taxi:** Readily available; the journey to central Bologna takes about 15 minutes, with fares averaging €20-25.

4. Turin Airport (TRN)

SCAN THE QR CODE

1. Open your device camera app.
2. Position the QR code in the camera frame.
3. Hold your phone steady.
4. Wait for the code to be recognized.
5. Once recognized, tap on the notification or follow the prompt to access the content or action associated with the Qr code

- **Location:** Approximately 16 kilometers (10 miles) north of Turin, in the Piedmont region.

- **Overview:** Also known as Sandro Pertini Airport, it serves as a gateway to Turin and the surrounding Alpine areas, making it ideal for both city explorers and winter sports enthusiasts.

Transportation to/from the Airport:
- **Train:** The GTT railway connects the airport to Turin's Dora Station in about 19 minutes. Tickets cost €3.
- **Bus:** SADEM buses run between the airport and Turin's city center, with tickets priced at €7 for a one-way trip.
- **Taxi:** Available outside the terminal; the ride to central Turin takes about 30 minutes, with fares around €30-35.

5. Verona Villafranca Airport (VRN)

30

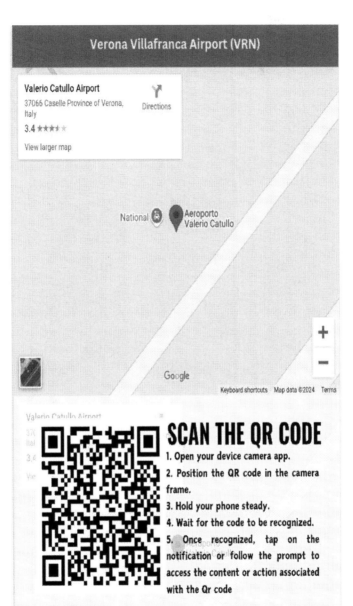

- **Location:** Approximately 10 kilometers (6 miles) southwest of Verona, in the Veneto region.

- **Overview:** Also known as Valerio Catullo Airport, it serves Verona and the surrounding areas, including Lake Garda.

Transportation to/from the Airport:
- **Bus:** The Aerobus service connects the airport to Verona Porta Nuova railway station in about 15 minutes. Tickets cost €6 for a one-way journey.
- **Taxi:** Available outside the terminal; a ride to central Verona takes approximately 15 minutes, with fares ranging from €15-20.

Contact Information:

- **Phone**: +39 045 809 5666
- **Website**: www.aeroportoverona.it

B. Transportation in the Northern Italy

Getting around Northern Italy is a breeze, thanks to its well-developed transportation network. Let's break down the best ways to get around.

1. Trains

If you want to travel quickly and comfortably, trains are the way to go. Northern Italy has an excellent rail system, with both high-speed and regional trains connecting major cities and smaller towns. The high-speed Frecciarossa and Italo trains are the fastest options, whisking you from Milan to Venice in just 2.5 hours or from Bologna to Florence in under 40 minutes. The trains are modern, with comfortable seating, free Wi-Fi, and even snack services on board.

For scenic routes, try taking a regional train through the Italian Alps or along the shores of Lake Como. Regional trains might be slower, but they offer stunning views of the countryside. You can buy tickets at the station, online, or via apps like Trenitalia or Italo, and prices range from €10-€70 depending on the route and class.

2. Buses

Buses are another great option, especially for reaching smaller towns and villages that don't have train stations. Companies like FlixBus and BusItalia offer long-distance routes between cities like Milan, Turin, and Verona at very affordable prices (as low as €5 if you book early!). Regional buses connect the more remote areas, like the picturesque villages in the Dolomites.

Buses can be slower than trains, but they often go to places that are harder to reach otherwise. They are also a budget-friendly choice for travelers looking to save a bit of money. You can buy tickets at bus stations, online, or directly from the driver in some cases.

3. Renting a Car

If you love the idea of exploring at your own pace, renting a car is a fantastic option. Northern Italy's road network is well-maintained, and the highways (or autostrade) are easy to navigate. Renting a car gives you the freedom to visit off-the-beaten-path locations, like the charming towns of Valpolicella wine country or the hidden beaches of Lake Garda.

However, keep in mind that driving in major cities like Milan or Venice can be tricky due to traffic and limited parking. Make sure to check for ZTL (Zona a Traffico Limitato) zones, where only local residents are allowed to drive. You can rent a car at the airport or in the city, with prices starting around €40 per day.

4. Boats and Ferries

If you're visiting Northern Italy's lakes or the coast, don't miss the chance to travel by boat. Ferries and water taxis are common on Lake Como, Lake Maggiore, and in Venice. It's a relaxing and scenic way to get around, with stunning views of the water and the surrounding landscapes. Ferry tickets usually cost between €5-€15, depending on the route.

5. Local Tips

In bigger cities like Milan, Venice, and Turin, you can also use the local metro, trams, and buses. Consider buying a day pass if you plan to use public transportation frequently—it will save you time and money. Most cities have user-friendly apps that help you find routes, schedules, and ticket options.

C. When to Visit

Northern Italy is incredible no matter when you go, but each season brings its own vibe and unique experiences. Let's break it down so you can choose the time that feels just right for your trip.

March to May

If you love mild weather, blooming flowers, and fewer crowds, spring is your season. Picture this: fields of wildflowers in the Italian countryside, warm days perfect for strolling through vineyards, and cozy evenings in charming piazzas. Temperatures hover between 50-70°F, making it ideal for outdoor adventures like hiking in the Dolomites or exploring the gardens of Lake Como.

Spring also marks the start of local festivals and events, like the Easter celebrations and the famous Vinitaly wine fair in Verona. It's a great time to experience the region's culture without the summer rush. Plus, with the lower prices on flights and hotels, it's a smart pick for travelers who want to enjoy the sights without breaking the bank.

June to August

Summer in Northern Italy is all about long sunny days, lively cities, and tons of outdoor activities. Imagine this: swimming in the sparkling waters of Lake Garda, hiking the stunning trails of the Italian Alps, or enjoying a sunset dinner by the canals of Venice. Temperatures range from 75-90°F, making it warm but perfect for enjoying the lakes, mountains, and coast.

This is also festival season—think open-air concerts, food festivals, and the iconic Venice Biennale. But here's the thing: it's the busiest time of year, so expect larger crowds and book your accommodations well in advance. If you don't mind the buzz, it's a fantastic time to soak up the energy and enjoy the lively atmosphere.

September to November

If you're a foodie or a wine lover, fall is when Northern Italy truly shines. As the temperatures cool down to a comfortable 50-70°F, the region comes alive with harvest season. Picture vineyards turning shades of gold and red, farmers' markets bursting with fresh produce, and wine tours in Piedmont and Valpolicella that let you sample the best of the season.

This is the time for truffle hunting in Alba, tasting the rich red wines of Barolo, and enjoying cozy meals at family-run trattorias. It's less crowded than summer, so you can explore at your own pace and enjoy the autumn colors in cities like Turin and Florence. It's a perfect time to experience the true flavor of Italy.

December to February

Dreaming of a snowy escape? Winter in Northern Italy is like stepping into a storybook, especially if you love winter sports or cozy mountain towns. The Italian Alps and Dolomites are a paradise for skiing, snowboarding, and snowshoeing. Imagine crisp mountain air, stunning snow-covered landscapes, and warm evenings spent by the fireplace with a glass of local grappa.

The cities have a different charm in winter too—Venice looks magical under a light fog, and Milan's Christmas markets light up the squares with festive cheer. It's cold, with temperatures ranging from 25-45°F, so pack warm clothes! But the good news? Fewer tourists and cheaper flights make it a great time for budget travelers.

So, When Should You Go?

It all depends on what kind of experience you're after. If you want warm weather and a lively atmosphere, go for summer. For beautiful scenery and delicious food, fall is your best bet. Spring is perfect if you want milder weather and fewer crowds, while winter offers a snowy adventure and a quieter, magical vibe.

D. Visa and Entry Requirements

Before you pack your bags and set off on your Northern Italy adventure, let's make sure you have everything in order for a smooth entry. Depending on your nationality, the visa requirements can vary, so here's what you need to know to avoid any surprises at the border.

1. Do You Need a Visa?

For most travelers from the United States, Canada, the United Kingdom, and many EU countries, a visa isn't required for short stays in Italy, as long as your trip is 90 days or less within a 180-day period. This rule applies for tourism, family visits, and business purposes. You'll only need a valid passport, which must be valid for at least three months beyond your planned departure date from the Schengen Area (which includes Italy).

If you're coming from Australia, New Zealand, Japan, or South Korea, the same rule generally applies—no visa needed for short visits of up to 90 days. However, make sure your passport is in good condition and has enough blank pages for entry and exit stamps.

For travelers from countries outside this list, such as those in Africa, Asia, and parts of South America, a Schengen visa may be required. The Schengen visa allows entry to 26 European countries, including Italy. It's best to check with the Italian consulate or embassy in your country for specific requirements and to apply well in advance of your trip.

2. ETIAS Travel Authorization (Starting 2025)

Starting in 2025, travelers from visa-exempt countries (like the U.S., Canada, and Australia) will need to apply for an ETIAS (European Travel Information and Authorization System) before visiting Italy. The ETIAS isn't a visa; it's more like an electronic travel authorization, similar to the ESTA for the U.S.

The process is straightforward: you fill out an online form, which takes about 10 minutes, and pay a small fee (around €7). You'll need your passport details and an email address to complete the application. Once approved, your ETIAS will be valid for three years or until your passport expires. Make sure to complete this step before your flight to avoid any last-minute issues.

3. Important Documents to Carry

When you arrive in Italy, the immigration officer may ask to see a few documents in addition to your passport:

- **Proof of Accommodation:** A hotel booking, Airbnb reservation, or a letter from a friend or family member you're staying with.
- **Return or Onward Ticket:** A ticket showing that you plan to leave the country within 90 days.
- **Proof of Financial Means:** This isn't always checked, but it's good to have a credit card or bank statement handy, just in case.
- **Travel Insurance:** While not always required, having proof of travel insurance that covers health emergencies is strongly recommended, especially for Schengen visa applicants.

4. Tips for a Smooth Entry

- **Double-Check Passport Validity:** Make sure your passport is valid for at least six months beyond your travel dates to avoid any issues.
- **Arrive Early at the Airport:** Lines at immigration can get long, especially

during peak travel seasons like summer and holidays.
- **Be Prepared for Questions:** The immigration officer might ask about your travel plans—where you're staying, how long you're visiting, and why you're traveling. Just answer honestly and confidently.
- **Keep Copies of Important Documents:** It's a good idea to have digital and physical copies of your passport, visa (if required), and travel insurance details.

E. Currency, Costs, and Budget Tips

Money matters can be one of the trickiest parts of travel, especially when you're visiting a new country. Here's what you need to know about handling money in Northern Italy, from understanding the local currency to getting the most value for your euro.

1. Currency: The Euro (€)

In Italy, the official currency is the euro (€). It's used across most of Europe, making it easy if you're traveling to multiple countries. The euro comes in both coins (€0.01 to €2) and banknotes (€5, €10, €20, €50, €100, and higher). Keep some small change handy for things like bus tickets, tips, and coffee, as many smaller shops and cafés prefer cash for low-cost items.

Before your trip, it's a good idea to check the current exchange rate to get an idea of how far your dollars, pounds, or other currencies will go. Rates fluctuate, but as of 2024, €1 is roughly equivalent to $1.10 USD or £0.85 GBP. It's best to exchange a small amount of cash before you leave, just to have on hand when you arrive.

2. Credit Cards and ATMs: How to Pay

Credit and debit cards are widely accepted across Northern Italy, especially in cities like Milan, Venice, and Turin. Visa and Mastercard are the most commonly accepted, but it's smart to have some cash on hand, particularly when visiting smaller towns, family-owned restaurants, or outdoor markets.

ATMs (bancomat) are easy to find and usually offer the best exchange rates. Most Italian ATMs don't charge a fee, but your home bank might, so check ahead. Stick to ATMs attached to banks for added security, and avoid using those in busy tourist areas, as they sometimes have higher fees or lower withdrawal limits.

- **Pro Tip**: Notify your bank of your travel plans before leaving to avoid any issues with your cards being blocked for suspicious activity.

3. Typical Costs: What to Expect

The cost of traveling in Northern Italy can vary depending on where you go and your travel style. Here's a rough idea of what you can expect to pay:

- **Accommodation**: Budget travelers can find hostel beds starting at €25-€50 per night. Mid-range hotels range from €100-€200 per night, while luxury options can go up to €500 or more in places like Milan and Venice.
- **Meals**: A simple meal at a local trattoria or café might cost €10-€20 per person, while a dinner at a nice restaurant can range from €30-€60. If you're splurging on a fine dining experience or Michelin-starred restaurant, expect to pay €100+ per person.
- **Transportation**: A train ride between major cities like Milan and Venice costs about €20-€50 for standard class, depending on the route and how early you book. Local buses and metro tickets typically cost €1.50-€2.50 each.
- **Activities:** Entry fees for major attractions like the Colosseum in Verona or the Milan Cathedral range from €10-€20. Day tours, wine tastings, or guided hikes usually start around €50-€100.

4. Budget Tips: Saving Money Without Sacrificing Experience

- **Travel Off-Peak:** Prices for flights, hotels, and tours are generally lower in the off-peak seasons (spring and fall). You'll avoid crowds and get better deals.
- **Use Public Transportation:** Instead of taxis, opt for the metro, buses, or trains. Italy's public transportation is efficient and much cheaper than taking a taxi, especially in big cities.
- **Eat Like a Local:** Skip the touristy restaurants and look for trattorias or osterias, where locals dine. These spots often have better prices and more authentic dishes.
- **Book in Advance**: For popular attractions and train tickets, booking online ahead of time can save you both time and money. Many places offer discounted rates for early reservations.
- **Get a City Pass:** Cities like Milan and Venice offer passes that include public transport and entry to multiple attractions at a reduced price. They can be a great value if you plan to do a lot of sightseeing.

5. Tipping and Gratuities

Tipping in Northern Italy is more laid-back compared to the U.S. It's not mandatory, but if you receive great service, it's always appreciated. Rounding up the bill or leaving a small tip of

5-10% at restaurants is typical. For taxis, it's common to round up to the nearest euro, and for hotel staff like porters, a tip of €1-€2 per bag is generous.

F. Travel Insurance and Safety Tips

1. Why You Need Travel Insurance

You might be thinking, "Do I really need travel insurance?" The answer is yes. Travel insurance is like a safety net that can cover you if things go wrong. From flight cancellations and lost luggage to unexpected health issues, a good insurance plan helps protect your investment and gives you peace of mind.

Medical care in Italy is excellent, but it can be costly for tourists. While EU residents can use their European Health Insurance Card (EHIC) for coverage, travelers from outside the EU, like those from the U.S., Canada, or Australia, will need separate insurance. Look for a policy that includes emergency medical care, trip cancellations, lost or stolen belongings, and 24/7 assistance.

- **Pro Tip:** Make sure your policy covers activities you plan to do, like skiing in the Alps or hiking in the Dolomites.

High-adrenaline sports may require extra coverage.

2. How to Choose the Right Insurance

There are many travel insurance providers, so choosing the right one can feel overwhelming. Here's what to look for in a good policy:

- **Medical Coverage:** Look for a minimum of €100,000 in medical coverage. This should cover hospital visits, emergency surgeries, and doctor's fees.
- **Trip Cancellation and Delay**: Ensure your policy covers trip cancellations due to unexpected events like illness, bad weather, or family emergencies.
- **Baggage and Personal Items:** Choose a policy that covers lost, damaged, or stolen luggage, including valuables like cameras or laptops.
- **24/7 Assistance:** This feature is important in case you need help coordinating medical care or rebooking flights in an emergency.

Popular insurance companies like World Nomads, Allianz, and Travel Guard offer comprehensive packages tailored to European travel. Be sure to compare policies and read the fine print before purchasing.

3. Safety Tips for a Smooth Trip

Northern Italy is generally very safe for tourists, but it's always wise to take a few precautions. Here's how to keep yourself and your belongings secure:

- **Watch for Pickpockets:** In busy tourist areas like Venice, Milan, and on crowded trains, pickpockets can be a problem. Keep your valuables close, use a money belt, and avoid flashing cash or expensive jewelry.
- **Use Official Taxis:** When traveling by taxi, use registered cabs or ride-hailing apps like Uber. This helps you avoid scams or being overcharged.
- **Be Aware of ZTL Zones:** Many Italian cities have ZTL (Zona a Traffico Limitato) areas where only local vehicles are allowed. If you're driving, make sure to check for these zones to avoid hefty fines.
- **Emergency Numbers:** In case of an emergency, dial 112, the general emergency number for police, ambulance, and fire services in Italy.

4. Health and COVID-19 Considerations

While Italy no longer has strict COVID-19 restrictions, it's a good idea to carry proof of vaccination or a negative test, as some places may still request it. Keep a small first-aid kit with you, including basic medications like painkillers, allergy medicine, and motion sickness pills if you plan to take boat rides on the lakes.

If you have any medical conditions, carry a note from your doctor detailing your health needs, especially if you need specific medications. Pharmacies (Farmacie) are easy to find and usually have a green cross sign. Pharmacists in Italy are knowledgeable and can help with minor health concerns or recommend over-the-counter medications.

5. Staying Connected and Informed

Download a reliable travel app like Google Maps, Rome2Rio, or Moovit for public transport navigation. These apps can help you find the best routes and avoid any areas with heavy traffic or unexpected delays.

Keep a list of important contacts, including your embassy, travel insurance provider, and emergency contacts back home. It's also a good idea to have a photocopy or digital version of your passport, insurance details, and any important documents in case they get lost or stolen.

G. Packing Essentials

1. Comfortable Shoes

Trust me on this—Northern Italy is best explored on foot, whether you're wandering through Milan's fashion districts, climbing the hills of Tuscany, or strolling the cobbled streets of Venice. Bring a pair of comfortable walking shoes that you can wear all day without blisters. If you plan to do any hiking in the Dolomites or around the lakes, pack lightweight hiking shoes with good grip. And don't forget a pair of stylish flats or sandals for evenings out; Italians love their fashion, and you might want to dress up a bit for dinner.

2. Weather-Appropriate Clothing

The weather in Northern Italy can be unpredictable, especially if you're visiting during the shoulder seasons of spring or fall. Layering is key! Here's a quick rundown of what to bring based on the season:

- **Spring (March-May):** Pack light sweaters, a good jacket, and a mix of short-sleeve and long-sleeve tops. Temperatures can range from 50-70°F, and a lightweight rain jacket or umbrella is a must—spring showers are common.
- **Summer (June-August):** Bring light, breathable clothing for the warm weather. Think T-shirts, shorts, sundresses, and a hat to protect against the sun. Temperatures can soar up to 90°F, so also pack sunscreen and sunglasses.

- **Fall (September-November):** You'll want layers—light sweaters, scarves, and a warm jacket—as temperatures range from 50-70°F but can drop quickly in the evenings. It's also harvest season, so bring a nice outfit if you plan on wine tasting in Piedmont.
- **Winter (December-February):** If you're heading to the mountains or planning to visit cities like Milan and Turin, pack a warm winter coat, gloves, and a hat. It can get quite cold, especially in the Alps, where temperatures can drop below freezing.

3. Daypack or Backpack

A sturdy daypack is a lifesaver for carrying all your essentials while exploring. Choose one that's big enough to fit your water bottle, snacks, a camera, and any souvenirs you pick up along the way. It's also great for keeping your hands free while navigating busy city streets or hiking trails.

4. Electronics

You'll want to document your trip, so make sure to pack a good camera or smartphone with a charger and a power bank for those long sightseeing days. Bring a universal power adapter, as Italy uses the European-style plugs (Type C, F, and L). If you plan on using your phone for navigation or translations, download an offline map of Northern Italy and the Google Translate app in advance.

5. Travel Documents and Money Essentials

This might seem obvious, but it's easy to forget something important in the rush of packing. Here's a quick checklist:

- Passport and Visa (if needed)
- Travel Insurance Details
- Copies of Important Documents (digital and physical copies)
- Credit Cards and Cash in Euros (€): While cards are widely accepted, it's good to have some cash on hand, especially for small purchases in markets or rural areas.

6. Toiletries and Health Essentials

Most of the basics are easy to find in Italy, but there are a few things you might want to bring from home, especially if you have specific preferences:

- **Medications and Prescriptions:** Bring enough for your entire trip, plus a little extra in case of delays.
- **Travel-Sized Toiletries:** Include shampoo, conditioner, toothpaste, and deodorant. A pack of facial wipes can be handy for freshening up on the go.

- **First-Aid Kit:** Include band-aids, pain relievers, allergy medication, and motion sickness pills if you plan to take any boat rides on the lakes.

7. Special Extras

There are a few extra items that can make your trip smoother and more enjoyable:

- **Reusable Water Bottle:** Italy's tap water is safe to drink, and many cities have public fountains where you can refill your bottle for free.
- **Umbrella or Rain Jacket:** Northern Italy can be rainy, especially in spring and fall.
- **Scarf or Shawl:** Useful for visiting churches, where covering your shoulders might be required, and for an extra layer in cooler weather.
- **Swimsuit:** If you're heading to the lakes or the coast, you'll definitely want to take a dip

Chapter 3 Top Destinations in Northern Italy

A. Venice

Hello there, traveler!

I can tell you're excited about Venice—the city that seems to float on water. It's a place where romance, history, and sheer beauty come together in the most magical way. Trust me, once you step off the train or boat, you'll feel like you've entered a dream. Let's take a stroll together through the wonders of Venice and make sure you soak in every unforgettable moment.

Where You Are: Venice, The Floating City

You're in Venice, one of the most unique cities in the world. Instead of roads, there are canals;

instead of cars, there are gondolas. The city spreads across 118 small islands connected by over 400 bridges, and every corner feels like a scene from a painting. It's a maze of narrow alleys, ancient buildings, and shimmering water that's unlike anywhere else you've ever been.

A Little Bit of History

Venice has a rich, captivating history. It was founded over 1,500 years ago by people escaping barbarian invasions. They built their homes on wooden stilts in the lagoon, creating a city that became a powerful maritime empire. During the Middle Ages and Renaissance, Venice was the gateway between Europe and the East, making it a wealthy trade hub. You can still see this legacy today in its magnificent palaces, churches, and art.

Walking through Venice, you'll notice the influence of Byzantine, Gothic, and Renaissance architecture. It's a living museum, and every building seems to have a story. The best part? You don't need a guidebook—just wander, and let the city's history reveal itself to you.

Must-See Sights

1. St. Mark's Square (Piazza San Marco):
This is Venice's grandest square, and it's always buzzing with life. Stop by the stunning St. Mark's Basilica with its golden mosaics and intricate

domes—it's a masterpiece of Byzantine architecture. Don't miss the Doge's Palace next door, where Venice's rulers once lived. For the best view of the city, head up to the Campanile (bell tower) and take in the breathtaking panorama.

2. The Grand Canal:
The Grand Canal is Venice's main waterway, winding its way through the city in a big, graceful curve. Take a vaporetto (water bus) or treat yourself to a gondola ride. You'll glide past historic palaces, charming houses, and the famous Rialto Bridge—it's like floating through Venice's history.

3. The Islands: Murano, Burano, and Torcello:
Want to see more than just the main city? Hop on a boat to Murano, where you can watch artisans create beautiful glass. Head to Burano for its brightly colored houses and lace-making shops—it's like stepping into a rainbow. And if you want a bit of peace, visit Torcello, one of the oldest parts of Venice, with its quiet, ancient church.

Where to Stay

No matter your budget, Venice has plenty of options:

- **Luxury**: Stay at the Gritti Palace, a historic hotel overlooking the Grand

Canal with incredible views and top-notch service.
- **Mid-Range**: Hotel Antiche Figure offers comfort and a fantastic location right by the train station.
- **Budget**: Check out Generator Venice, a trendy hostel on the island of Giudecca with a fun atmosphere and great city views.

What to Eat and Drink

Venetian cuisine is all about fresh, local ingredients and flavors you won't find anywhere else. Start your day with a cappuccino at a café in St. Mark's Square. For lunch, try sarde in saor (sweet and sour sardines) or bigoli in salsa (a traditional pasta dish with anchovy sauce). Don't forget to visit a bacaro (Venetian wine bar) for cicchetti—small bites like crostini and fried seafood, paired perfectly with a glass of Veneto wine or an Aperol spritz.

Best Time to Visit

Venice is magical year-round, but here's what to expect:

- **Spring (March-May)**: Mild weather and blooming flowers make this a wonderful time to visit without the summer crowds.
- **Summer (June-August)**: The city is lively, and it's the best time for boat rides and

gelato by the canal. It can get busy, so book ahead!
- **Fall (September-November):** The weather cools down, and the crowds thin out. It's also a great time for food lovers, with autumnal dishes and wine harvest celebrations.
- **Winter (December-February):** The city feels quieter and more romantic. Visit during Carnival for masked balls and parades—it's like stepping back in time.

Good-to-Know Tips

- **Language:** While most Venetians speak Italian, many also understand English. A simple "Grazie" (thank you) goes a long way!
- **Currency:** You'll be using euros (€). Credit cards are widely accepted, but it's good to have some cash for small purchases.
- **Getting Around:** Venice is a walking city, so bring comfy shoes. For longer distances, use the vaporetto or try a gondola ride for a unique experience.

B. Milan

Hello there, stylish traveler!

I see you've made it to Milan, and let me tell you—you're in for a treat! Milan isn't just another city on your travel list; it's the vibrant heart of Northern Italy, where fashion, art, and history come together in the most incredible way. This is a place where centuries-old architecture stands proudly beside cutting-edge design, and where every street has a story. Let's dive into Milan together and discover its must-see spots and hidden gems.

Where You Are: Milan, The Fashion Capital

You're in Milan, the fashion capital of the world, known for its glamorous boutiques, historic landmarks, and bustling piazzas. This city is fast-paced, stylish, and full of energy, yet it still holds onto its rich heritage. It's a place where you can sip an espresso in a centuries-old café, then step into a sleek designer store just a few steps away. Milan is a city that moves forward while keeping one foot firmly in the past.

A Little Bit of History

Milan's history is as fascinating as it gets. It was once the capital of the Western Roman Empire, and you can still see traces of its ancient past in the city's ruins. Fast forward to the Renaissance, and Milan became a hub of art and culture, attracting masters like Leonardo da Vinci, who left his mark with works like "The Last Supper." Today, Milan is Italy's economic powerhouse, blending its storied past with a modern, cosmopolitan vibe.

Must-See Sights

1. The Duomo di Milano:
This stunning cathedral is Milan's crown jewel, and trust me—you won't believe your eyes. The Duomo di Milano is one of the largest Gothic cathedrals in the world, with over 3,000 statues adorning its intricate façade. Climb up to the rooftop for an unforgettable view of the city, where you can see the Alps on a clear day. It's pure magic.

2. The Last Supper (Cenacolo Vinciano):
You can't visit Milan without seeing Leonardo da Vinci's masterpiece, The Last Supper, housed in the Santa Maria delle Grazie church. It's one of

the most famous paintings in the world, depicting the dramatic moment when Jesus announces his betrayal. Book your tickets well in advance, as spots fill up quickly—it's a once-in-a-lifetime experience.

3. Galleria Vittorio Emanuele II:
Step into Italy's oldest shopping mall, a breathtaking arcade filled with luxury shops, charming cafés, and beautiful mosaic floors. This is the place to indulge in a bit of shopping or simply grab a cappuccino and people-watch. Don't forget to spin on the bull mosaic in the center for good luck!

4. Sforza Castle (Castello Sforzesco):
Explore the grand Sforza Castle, a symbol of Milan's power and prestige. Today, it houses several museums, including collections of ancient art and a stunning unfinished sculpture by Michelangelo. It's a great spot for a leisurely stroll through history, surrounded by beautiful gardens.

Where to Stay

Milan has accommodation options for every budget:

- **Luxury:** Stay at the Hotel Principe di Savoia, an iconic hotel known for its elegance and impeccable service.

- **Mid-Range:** Check out NH Milano Touring, offering comfort and style near the city center.
- **Budget:** For a wallet-friendly option, Ostello Bello is a fun and cozy hostel with a great location and friendly atmosphere.

What to Eat and Drink

Get ready to savor some of Milan's best dishes. Start your culinary adventure with risotto alla Milanese, a creamy saffron-infused risotto that's pure comfort on a plate. Try ossobuco, a tender veal shank cooked slowly with vegetables—it's a Milanese classic. And don't leave without indulging in a slice of panettone, especially if you visit during the holiday season.

When it comes to drinks, Milan is famous for its aperitivo culture. Head to the trendy Navigli district for a glass of Negroni or an Aperol Spritz as the sun sets. The vibe is lively, and the drinks often come with a generous spread of snacks, making it the perfect way to start your evening.

Best Time to Visit

Milan is fantastic year-round, but here's what to expect:

- **Spring (March-May):** Mild temperatures and blooming flowers make it a lovely time to explore the city.

- **Summer (June-August):** It's hot, but the city buzzes with events like Milan Fashion Week and open-air concerts. Be prepared for crowds!
- **Fall (September-November):** The weather cools down, and the city comes alive with art exhibitions and wine tastings.
- **Winter (December-February):** Milan turns festive with Christmas markets and light displays. It's also a great time for sales if you love shopping.

C. Florence

Welcome to Florence, the birthplace of the Renaissance—a city that's like stepping back in time to an era of incredible art, architecture, and history. As you walk its cobblestone streets, it feels like the entire city is a museum. Trust me, Florence is a place where you'll want to stop and soak it all in, from the incredible sculptures to the stunning frescoes. Let's dive into what makes this city so unforgettable and why it's a must-visit on your Northern Italy journey.

Where You Are: The Heart of Tuscany

You're in Florence, the capital of Tuscany, nestled in the rolling hills of central Italy. This city was once the powerhouse of art and culture, home to legends like Michelangelo, Leonardo da Vinci, and Dante Alighieri. Florence's influence during the Renaissance can still be felt today—every building and square seems to have a piece of history attached to it. The city is compact and walkable, making it easy to explore on foot.

Must-See Sights

1. The Duomo (Cathedral of Santa Maria del Fiore):
You can't miss the Duomo—its red-tiled dome dominates the Florence skyline. Designed by Filippo Brunelleschi, the cathedral is a masterpiece of Gothic architecture. Climb up the 463 steps to the top of the dome for a breathtaking view of the city. Inside, you'll find beautiful frescoes, including Vasari's Last Judgment. It's one of those experiences that will stay with you long after you leave.

2. The Uffizi Gallery:
Art lovers, this one's for you. The Uffizi Gallery houses one of the most impressive collections of Renaissance art in the world. You'll see works by Botticelli (don't miss "The Birth of Venus"), Titian,

and Caravaggio. The museum can get busy, so it's a good idea to book your tickets in advance. Even if you're not a big art buff, the sheer beauty of these masterpieces will leave you in awe.

3. Ponte Vecchio:

Stroll across the Ponte Vecchio, Florence's most iconic bridge. This medieval stone bridge is lined with charming shops selling jewelry, art, and souvenirs. It's the perfect spot to take in the sunset over the Arno River. Fun fact: The bridge is one of the few in Florence that wasn't destroyed during World War II, thanks to an order from Hitler himself.

What to Eat and Drink

Florence is a food lover's paradise, so make sure you come hungry. Start with bistecca alla Fiorentina, a thick, juicy T-bone steak cooked to perfection—it's a Florentine specialty you can't miss. For a lighter bite, try ribollita, a hearty vegetable and bread soup that's perfect on a chilly day. Don't forget to grab a scoop of gelato at one of the city's famous gelaterias—Vivoli or Gelateria dei Neri are local favorites.

For drinks, enjoy a glass of Chianti wine, made from the vineyards just outside the city. It pairs perfectly with any Tuscan meal and gives you a true taste of the region.

Best Time to Visit

Florence is beautiful year-round, but here's what to expect during different seasons:

- **Spring (March-May):** The city comes alive with blooming flowers and mild weather—ideal for sightseeing without the summer crowds.
- **Summer (June-August):** It's hot and bustling with tourists. Be prepared for long lines at major attractions, but the vibrant atmosphere and outdoor events are worth it.
- **Fall (September-November):** This is a fantastic time for foodies, as it's harvest season. The weather is cooler, and the city's wine bars are buzzing.
- **Winter (December-February):** It's quieter, making it a great time to visit museums and cozy up in local trattorias. Plus, the city looks magical during the holiday season.

D. Lake Como

Welcome to Lake Como, one of the most beautiful and luxurious destinations in Northern Italy. This isn't just any lake—it's a place where the Alps meet the sparkling waters, and charming villages dot the shoreline. You've probably seen the photos of its crystal-clear waters and grand villas, but trust me, seeing it in person is something else entirely. Let's explore Lake Como together and find out why it's a favorite getaway for celebrities, nature lovers, and anyone looking for a bit of peace and elegance.

Where You Are: The Jewel of the Italian Lakes

You're in the heart of the Italian lake district, about an hour's drive north of Milan. Lake Como is shaped like an upside-down Y, with three main branches: Como, Lecco, and Colico. The lake is surrounded by steep hills and mountains, making it feel like a secret hideaway. Each town around the lake has its own charm, from the lively streets of Como to the quiet elegance of Bellagio, often called the "Pearl of the Lake."

Must-See Sights

1. Bellagio: The Pearl of Lake Como

If you only visit one place around Lake Como, make it Bellagio. This picturesque town sits right at the intersection of the lake's three branches, offering panoramic views in every direction. Stroll along the waterfront promenade, explore the narrow cobblestone streets, and visit Villa Melzi Gardens for a peaceful escape. Bellagio is also a great spot for shopping—you'll find lovely boutiques selling silk scarves, ceramics, and local wines.

2. Villa del Balbianello: A Hollywood Favorite

You might recognize Villa del Balbianello from movies like Star Wars: Episode II and Casino Royale. Perched on a wooded peninsula, this stunning villa offers breathtaking views of the lake and lush terraced gardens. Take a guided tour to learn about its fascinating history and the explorer who once owned it. You can reach the villa by boat, which makes for a scenic and memorable trip.

3. The Town of Como: Gateway to the Lake

Start your Lake Como adventure in the town of Como, the lake's namesake. It's a lively spot filled with shops, cafés, and historical sites. Don't miss the Como Cathedral, a beautiful Gothic building that's one of the region's finest. For the best view of the lake, take the funicular up to Brunate—a tiny hilltop village where you can look out over the entire lake and beyond to the Swiss Alps.

What to Do at Lake Como

Whether you're looking for relaxation or adventure, there's plenty to do at Lake Como. Rent a speedboat for a day and zip across the water, stopping at various villages and villas along the way. If you're into hiking, there are fantastic trails with views that will leave you speechless, like the Greenway del Lago di Como, which winds along the western shore.

For a more laid-back experience, just grab a gelato and find a quiet spot by the water. The gentle sound of the waves, the view of the mountains, and the fresh lake breeze—it's pure bliss.

Where to Stay

From luxury hotels to charming B&Bs, there's a place for every type of traveler:

- **Luxury:** Stay at the iconic Grand Hotel Tremezzo, a 5-star hotel with stunning lake views, a floating pool, and top-notch service.

- **Mid-Range:** Check out Hotel Du Lac in Bellagio, offering comfortable rooms and a great location right on the waterfront.
- **Budget:** For a more affordable option, La Locanda del Cantiere in Laglio provides cozy rooms with lake views and a friendly atmosphere.

What to Eat and Drink

Lake Como's cuisine is as delightful as its scenery. Start with missoltini, a traditional dish of sun-dried lake fish, or try risotto al pesce persico, a creamy risotto topped with freshly caught perch. If you're a cheese lover, don't miss the local taleggio—it's rich, creamy, and pairs perfectly with a glass of wine from the Lombardy region.

Speaking of wine, enjoy a glass of Nebbiolo or Valtellina Superiore, both excellent choices that come from vineyards just north of the lake. And for dessert? Treat yourself to a slice of miascia, a local cake made with apples and berries.

Best Time to Visit

Lake Como is beautiful year-round, but here's what each season offers:

- **Spring (March-May):** The flowers bloom, and the weather is mild—perfect for hiking and exploring the gardens.

- **Summer (June-August):** It's the peak season, with warm weather ideal for boating and swimming. It's lively, but expect more tourists.
- **Fall (September-November):** The crowds thin out, and the fall colors are spectacular. It's a wonderful time for wine tasting and relaxing by the lake.
- **Winter (December-February):** It's quieter and more peaceful. You'll find fewer tourists, and it's a cozy time to enjoy the lakeside villages without the crowds.

E. Cinque Terre

Welcome to Cinque Terre, one of the most enchanting places you'll find along the Italian Riviera. Imagine five vibrant, cliffside villages nestled between the sparkling Mediterranean Sea and steep, terraced hills covered in vineyards. The name Cinque Terre literally means "Five Lands," and each village has its own unique charm. Whether you're here for the breathtaking views, the fresh seafood, or the hiking trails that connect it all, Cinque Terre is the perfect blend of natural beauty and Italian tradition. Let's explore this coastal paradise together!

Where You Are

You're in the heart of the Liguria region, along the stunning stretch of coastline known as the Italian Riviera. Cinque Terre is made up of five villages: Monterosso al Mare, Vernazza, Corniglia, Manarola, and Riomaggiore. They're perched on the cliffs, with colorful houses that seem to spill down into the blue sea. The villages are connected by hiking trails, boats, and a small regional train, making it easy to hop from one to the next. This place is all about slowing down, savoring the views, and enjoying la dolce vita.

Must-See Villages

1. Monterosso al Mare:
Monterosso is the largest of the five villages and the best spot for beach lovers. Here, you'll find sandy shores and crystal-clear waters perfect for a swim. Wander through the old town, where you can visit the Church of San Giovanni Battista and sample local lemon products—Monterosso is famous for its sweet limoncino liqueur. Don't leave without trying the anchovies, a regional specialty that's much tastier than you might think!

2. Vernazza:

Vernazza is often considered the most picturesque village in Cinque Terre. The tiny harbor is framed by colorful buildings, and there's a charming little piazza where you can sip an espresso and watch the boats bobbing in the water. Climb up to the Doria Castle for a spectacular view of the village and the coastline. It's the perfect spot for sunset photos.

3. Manarola:
Manarola is the oldest village in Cinque Terre, and its charm is undeniable. The pastel-colored houses are perched on a cliff, and it's a popular spot for cliff diving. Take a stroll down the Via dell'Amore, a scenic path that connects Manarola to Riomaggiore. It's a short, easy walk, but the views of the sea are unforgettable. Be sure to try a glass of the local Sciacchetrà wine, made from grapes grown on the steep terraces.

What to Do in Cinque Terre

Hiking the Cinque Terre Trails:
One of the best ways to experience Cinque Terre is by hiking the trails that link the villages. The most famous is the Sentiero Azzurro (Blue Trail), which offers stunning coastal views and takes you through vineyards, olive groves, and charming villages. The trail can be challenging in parts, so wear good walking shoes and bring plenty of water.

Take a Boat Tour:

Seeing Cinque Terre from the water is a must. Hop on a boat tour to get a different perspective of the colorful villages and dramatic cliffs. It's a relaxing way to soak in the beauty of the coastline, and you might even spot dolphins along the way.

Enjoy the Local Food:

Cinque Terre is a food lover's paradise. Start with pesto alla genovese, a local specialty made with fresh basil, pine nuts, garlic, and Parmesan cheese. Try it with trofie pasta for an authentic experience. Seafood is the star here—don't miss the chance to try spaghetti alle vongole (spaghetti with clams) or fritto misto (a mix of fried seafood) at a seaside trattoria.

Best Time to Visit

Cinque Terre is stunning year-round, but here's what to expect during each season:

- **Spring (March-May):** The weather is mild, and the flowers are in full bloom. It's perfect for hiking and exploring without the summer crowds.
- **Summer (June-August):** The busiest season, with warm temperatures and lots of visitors. It's ideal for beach activities, but be prepared for packed trains and trails.
- **Fall (September-October):** The crowds thin out, and the weather is still pleasant.

It's also harvest season for the vineyards, so you might catch some local wine festivals.
- **Winter (November-February):** It's the quietest time of year, and some trails may be closed. However, the villages are peaceful, and you'll get a more authentic feel of local life.

Where to Stay

Cinque Terre has accommodations for every budget:

- **Luxury:** Stay at Hotel Porto Roca in Monterosso for incredible views and direct access to the beach.
- **Mid-Range:** Try La Torretta Lodge in Manarola, a charming boutique hotel with beautiful terraces.
- **Budget:** Check out Affittacamere Edi in Riomaggiore for affordable, comfortable rooms close to the main attractions.

F. Turin

Welcome to Turin, one of Northern Italy's most underrated gems. If you're looking for a city that's rich in history, filled with grand architecture, and buzzing with culture, you're in the right place. Turin might not have the crowds of Venice or the glamour of Milan, but it's the kind of place that will surprise you at every turn. It's a city of elegant boulevards, majestic palaces, and the perfect blend of old-world charm and modern energy. Let's explore Turin together and uncover why it's such a special place.

Where You Are: The Capital of Piedmont

You've arrived in Turin (or Torino, as the locals call it), the capital of the Piedmont region. Nestled at the foot of the Alps, Turin offers stunning mountain views, especially on clear days. This city was once the first capital of unified Italy and is home to the House of Savoy, Italy's royal family. Today, it's known for its sophisticated style, innovative spirit, and love for all things chocolate and coffee.

Must-See Sights

1. The Mole Antonelliana:
This is Turin's most iconic landmark and a must-see on your visit. Originally designed as a synagogue, the Mole Antonelliana now houses the National Cinema Museum—a fantastic spot for movie buffs. Take the glass elevator up to the top for a panoramic view of the entire city and

the snow-capped Alps in the distance. It's breathtaking and a great photo op.

2. Piazza Castello and the Royal Palace:

Turin's heart beats in Piazza Castello, a grand square surrounded by elegant buildings. Here, you'll find the Royal Palace of Turin, once the residence of the Savoy kings. Step inside to explore opulent rooms filled with stunning artwork and historical artifacts. Don't miss the Armeria Reale, one of the best collections of ancient arms and armor in Europe.

3. The Egyptian Museum (Museo Egizio):

Did you know that Turin is home to the second-largest Egyptian museum in the world? It's an absolute must-visit, with thousands of artifacts that date back over 5,000 years. The mummies, statues, and ancient relics will transport you to a different era. Even if you're not a history buff, this place is fascinating.

What to Eat and Drink

Turin is the food capital of the Piedmont region, famous for its rich, hearty cuisine. Start with a plate of agnolotti, small pasta pockets stuffed with meat, served with butter and sage. For something truly special, try bagna càuda, a warm dip made of garlic, anchovies, and olive oil, served with fresh vegetables—perfect for a cozy dinner.

And let's not forget about Turin's chocolate. This city is the birthplace of gianduiotto, a creamy hazelnut chocolate that's an absolute delight. Visit one of the local cafés and order a bicerin, a layered drink made with espresso, chocolate, and cream—it's pure heaven in a glass.

Best Time to Visit

Turin has its own charm in every season, so here's what to expect:

- **Spring (March-May):** The city starts to bloom, and the weather is mild. It's a lovely time to visit the parks and outdoor cafés.
- **Summer (June-August):** It can get warm, but it's also when the city is lively with events and festivals. It's a great time for exploring the nearby wine regions.
- **Fall (September-November):** This is harvest season, and the surrounding countryside is full of truffle hunts and wine tastings. The city itself is beautiful, with crisp air and colorful leaves.
- **Winter (December-February):** Turin feels like a winter wonderland during the holiday season. The Christmas lights and markets give the city a magical atmosphere, and the nearby Alps offer fantastic skiing.

Where to Stay

Turin has a wide range of accommodations to fit your budget:

- **Luxury:** Stay at the Principi di Piemonte, an elegant hotel known for its classic Italian style and stunning views.
- **Mid-Range:** Check out NH Torino Santo Stefano, located right in the heart of the city with easy access to all the major sights.
- **Budget:** For a more affordable option, Bamboo Eco Hostel offers a cozy and friendly atmosphere.

G. Verona

Hello there, romantic traveler!

You've just stepped into Verona, a city where history and romance are intertwined in the most beautiful way. Verona is famous for being the setting of Shakespeare's Romeo and Juliet, but there's so much more to discover here. Picture medieval streets, ancient Roman ruins, and lively piazzas buzzing with life. Verona is one of those places that sweeps you off your feet from the moment you arrive. Let's dive into this enchanting city together and make sure you don't miss a single highlight.

Where You Are

You're in Verona, located in the Veneto region, just a short train ride from Venice. This charming city lies along the banks of the Adige River and is surrounded by vineyards and rolling hills. Verona is known for its well-preserved Roman architecture, Renaissance art, and, of course, its association with one of the greatest love stories ever told. Whether you're a history lover, a foodie, or just here for the romantic vibes, Verona has something special in store for you.

Must-See Sights

1. Juliet's House (Casa di Giulietta):
Start your visit with a little romance at Juliet's House, one of the most popular attractions in Verona. The iconic balcony, said to be where Juliet called out to Romeo, is a must-see. You can even step onto the balcony for a photo! Inside the house, you'll find a small museum filled with period furniture and Shakespearean memorabilia. Before you leave, don't forget to rub the statue of Juliet for good luck in love.

2. The Verona Arena:

The Verona Arena is an ancient Roman amphitheater that dates back to the 1st century AD. It's one of the best-preserved arenas in Italy and is still used today for concerts and operas. Imagine sitting under the stars, listening to a live opera in the same place where gladiators once fought. It's an unforgettable experience and a true highlight of any trip to Verona.

3. Piazza delle Erbe:

This lively square is the heart of Verona's social scene. It's surrounded by colorful medieval buildings, and the market here sells everything from fresh produce to local crafts. Grab a seat at a café, order an Aperol Spritz, and take in the atmosphere. Nearby, you'll find the Torre dei Lamberti—climb to the top for a fantastic view of the city.

What to Eat and Drink

Verona's food scene is all about hearty, flavorful dishes made with local ingredients. Start your meal with bigoli pasta, a thick spaghetti often served with duck or sardine sauce. Another local favorite is risotto all'Amarone, made with the region's famous Amarone wine—it's rich, creamy, and unforgettable. If you're a meat lover, try pastissada de caval, a traditional horse meat stew that's been a Veronese specialty for centuries.

For dessert, you can't go wrong with a slice of pandoro, a sweet, fluffy cake that's especially popular during the holiday season. Pair it with a glass of Recioto della Valpolicella, a sweet red wine from the nearby vineyards—it's the perfect end to a delicious meal.

Best Time to Visit

Verona is magical year-round, but here's what each season brings:

- **Spring (March-May):** The city comes alive with blooming flowers and outdoor events. It's a great time for sightseeing and exploring without the summer crowds.
- **Summer (June-August):** This is the peak season, especially when the Verona Opera Festival is in full swing. The weather is warm, and the city is buzzing with activity. Be prepared for crowds, especially around the major attractions.
- **Fall (September-November):** The weather cools down, and the vineyards around Verona are at their best. It's the perfect time for wine tasting and enjoying the autumn colors.
- **Winter (December-February):** The city feels cozy and festive, especially with the Christmas markets in Piazza delle Erbe. It's a quieter time to visit, but the charm of Verona is still in full swing.

Where to Stay

From luxurious hotels to charming B&Bs, Verona has something for every traveler:

- **Luxury:** Stay at the Due Torri Hotel, a historic 5-star hotel known for its elegant rooms and unbeatable location near Juliet's House.
- **Mid-Range:** Check out Hotel Milano & Spa, which offers a rooftop terrace with stunning views of the Verona Arena.
- **Budget:** For a cozy, affordable stay, try Romeo & Juliet B&B, a charming guesthouse just steps from the city center.

H. Bologna

Hello there, food lover!

Welcome to Bologna, a city that will win your heart (and stomach) from the very first bite. Known as La Grassa (The Fat One) for its incredible cuisine, Bologna is the capital of the Emilia-Romagna region and Italy's undisputed food capital. This is the birthplace of famous dishes like tagliatelle al ragù (better known as spaghetti Bolognese, though the locals might scold you for saying that!), mortadella, and rich, creamy lasagna. But there's so much more to Bologna than just food. It's a vibrant, historic city with medieval towers, red-brick buildings, and a buzzing, youthful energy thanks to its world-renowned university. Let's take a bite out of Bologna and discover why this city is a must-visit in Northern Italy.

Where You Are: The Heart of Emilia-Romagna

You're in Bologna, a city that's rightfully proud of its food, history, and culture. It's the capital of the Emilia-Romagna region, one of Italy's richest culinary areas. Bologna is famous for its porticos, which stretch for miles, providing shade in the summer and shelter in the winter. The city is also known for its deep-red buildings and towers, giving it the nickname La Rossa (The Red One). Beyond the food, Bologna has a rich intellectual history—it's home to Europe's oldest university, founded in 1088, which gives the city a youthful, lively feel.

Must-See Sights

1. Piazza Maggiore and the Basilica di San Petronio:
Start your exploration in Piazza Maggiore, the main square and the beating heart of Bologna. Here, you'll find the grand Basilica di San Petronio, one of the largest churches in the world. It's famous for its unfinished façade and its incredible interior, including a sundial that's the largest in the world. Sit at one of the outdoor cafés and watch the world go by—it's the perfect place to soak in the local atmosphere.

2. The Two Towers (Le Due Torri):
Bologna was once filled with hundreds of medieval towers, and the Two Towers—Torre Asinelli and Torre Garisenda—are the most iconic ones that remain. Climb the 498 steps of Torre Asinelli for a breathtaking view of the city's red rooftops and the surrounding countryside. It's a bit of a workout, but the view from the top is totally worth it!

3. Bologna's Porticos:
Bologna's porticos are a UNESCO World Heritage Site, and they're a unique feature of the city. These covered walkways stretch for over 24 miles, providing shelter and a beautiful place to stroll, shop, or enjoy a coffee. One of the most famous stretches is the Portico di San Luca, which leads up to the Sanctuary of the Madonna di San Luca on a hill overlooking the city.

What to Eat and Drink

Bologna is a paradise for food lovers, so make sure you come hungry! Start with a plate of tagliatelle al ragù, the original version of what we call spaghetti Bolognese. The rich, slow-cooked meat sauce is served with wide, flat tagliatelle pasta—it's a comforting dish you'll never forget.

For something quick, grab a slice of mortadella at a local deli or order a piadina, a delicious flatbread stuffed with cheese, meats, and veggies. Don't leave without trying tortellini in brodo, tiny pasta filled with meat and cheese, served in a savory broth—it's a local favorite.

When it comes to dessert, indulge in a slice of torta di riso, a traditional rice cake, or a scoop of gelato from one of Bologna's famous gelaterias, like Cremeria Funivia.

To drink, try a glass of Lambrusco, a slightly sparkling red wine from the region, or finish your meal with a shot of espresso—it's the perfect pick-me-up before you head out for more exploring.

Best Time to Visit

Bologna is vibrant year-round, but here's what you can expect from each season:

- **Spring (March-May):** The weather is mild, and the city is full of blooming flowers. It's a great time for walking tours and outdoor dining.
- **Summer (June-August):** The city can get hot, but it's also when the outdoor food markets and festivals are at their best. Many locals head to the coast, so you'll find fewer crowds in the city itself.
- **Fall (September-November):** This is harvest season, and the food scene is at its peak. It's the perfect time for truffle tastings and enjoying hearty autumn dishes.
- **Winter (December-February):** It's quieter and cozier, with festive Christmas markets and hearty comfort foods to warm you up. It's a great time to experience Bologna like a local.

Where to Stay

No matter your budget, Bologna has a place for you:

- **Luxury**: Stay at the elegant Grand Hotel Majestic "Già Baglioni", a historic hotel with beautifully decorated rooms and a prime location near Piazza Maggiore.
- **Mid-Range**: Hotel Metropolitan offers stylish, comfortable rooms with a rooftop terrace that's perfect for an evening drink.

- **Budget:** For an affordable stay, try Il Nosadillo, a friendly hostel with a great location and a welcoming vibe.

Chapter 4: Hidden Gems and Off-the-Beaten-Path Destinations

A. Exploring the Quiet Villages of the Dolomites

Welcome to the Dolomites, a place where jagged mountain peaks touch the sky and charming villages nestle quietly in the valleys below. If you're looking to escape the crowds and discover a side of Northern Italy that feels like a hidden paradise, then exploring the villages of the Dolomites is the perfect adventure for you. Imagine cozy wooden chalets, alpine meadows bursting with wildflowers, and locals who greet you with a warm smile. Let's take a stroll through this breathtaking landscape and uncover the hidden gems that make the Dolomites so special.

Where You Are

You're deep in the Dolomites, part of the Italian Alps and a UNESCO World Heritage site. This region is famous for its dramatic landscapes—towering limestone peaks, crystal-clear lakes, and lush green valleys. While many visitors flock to the popular ski resorts, there's a quieter, more authentic side of the Dolomites waiting to be discovered. The small villages scattered throughout the area offer a glimpse into traditional alpine life, far from the hustle and bustle of the tourist hotspots.

Must-Visit Villages

1. Ortisei (Urtijëi):
Nestled in the heart of the Val Gardena, Ortisei is a picture-perfect village known for its vibrant culture and stunning scenery. The town's streets are lined with traditional Tyrolean-style buildings, each decorated with colorful murals and flower-filled balconies. Stop by the local woodcarving shops—this craft has been a part of Ortisei's heritage for centuries. Take the Seceda cable car for jaw-dropping views of the surrounding peaks, or enjoy a peaceful walk through the pine forests that surround the village.

2. San Candido (Innichen):
If you're seeking charm and tranquility, San Candido is the place to be. This small village is known for its historic churches, including the Collegiate Church of San Candido, one of the

oldest in the region. The village is also a gateway to the Tre Cime di Lavaredo, three iconic peaks that are a favorite among hikers and photographers. Grab a bite at a local café and try a slice of apple strudel—it's a classic treat that perfectly captures the flavors of the Dolomites.

3. Cortina d'Ampezzo:
While it's more well-known than some of the other villages, Cortina d'Ampezzo still offers a taste of alpine luxury without the overwhelming crowds. Known as the "Queen of the Dolomites," Cortina is surrounded by majestic peaks and offers fantastic hiking and skiing opportunities. Stroll through the chic town center, filled with boutique shops and cafés, or take a scenic drive along the Great Dolomites Road for unforgettable views.

What to Do in the Dolomites

There's no shortage of activities in the Dolomites, whether you're here in summer or winter. In the warmer months, the hiking trails are endless, with options ranging from gentle walks through alpine meadows to challenging climbs up rocky peaks. The Alpe di Siusi (Seiser Alm) is a must-visit—this high-altitude meadow is the largest in Europe and offers spectacular views.

In the winter, the Dolomites transform into a snowy wonderland. Head to one of the smaller ski areas, like Val di Fassa, for a more relaxed experience. It's the perfect spot for skiing, snowshoeing, or simply sipping hot chocolate in a cozy mountain hut.

Where to Stay

The villages in the Dolomites offer a range of accommodations, from family-run guesthouses to luxurious mountain lodges:

- **Luxury:** Stay at Hotel Adler Dolomiti in Ortisei for a mix of comfort, spa amenities, and stunning views of the mountains.
- **Mid-Range**: Residence Ariston in San Candido offers charming apartments with easy access to hiking trails and the village center.
- **Budget**: For a more affordable stay, try Garni Maria in Cortina d'Ampezzo, a welcoming B&B with a friendly atmosphere.

B. Discovering the Prosecco Hills

If you're looking to experience the true taste of Northern Italy, then you've come to the right place: the Prosecco Hills. This area isn't just about stunning landscapes; it's where the magic of Italy's sparkling wine comes to life. Imagine rolling hills covered with rows of grapevines, historic villages perched on hilltops, and small, family-run wineries welcoming you with a smile and a glass of bubbly. Let's take a journey through the Prosecco Hills together and sip on the sparkling flavors that have made this region famous.

Where You Are: Veneto's Sparkling Wine Region

You're in the heart of the Prosecco DOCG region, stretching from Conegliano to Valdobbiadene. It's located just an hour's drive north of Venice, making it an easy and scenic day trip if you're visiting the city. The hills here are part of the UNESCO World Heritage list, recognized for their breathtaking beauty and cultural significance. This is where the famous Glera grape is grown, producing the world-renowned Prosecco wine. The region offers a mix of history, nature, and of course, delicious wine tasting experiences.

Must-Visit Spots in the Prosecco Hills

1. Valdobbiadene:
This charming town is at the heart of Prosecco production. It's surrounded by vineyards and offers stunning views of the hills. Start your day with a visit to a local winery, like Cantina Nino Franco, one of the oldest and most respected producers in the area. Here, you can tour the vineyards, learn about the Prosecco-making process, and enjoy a tasting session that will

leave you with a newfound appreciation for sparkling wine.

2. Conegliano:
Known as the gateway to the Prosecco Hills, Conegliano is a historic town with deep roots in winemaking. Visit the Conegliano Wine School, Italy's oldest wine-making school, and stroll through the town's picturesque streets. Don't miss the Castle of Conegliano, where you can enjoy panoramic views while sipping a chilled glass of Prosecco.

3. Strada del Prosecco (Prosecco Wine Road):
This scenic route winds through the rolling hills, taking you past vineyards, quaint villages, and countless wineries. It's a perfect drive for wine lovers, offering plenty of opportunities to stop and sample local Prosecco. Consider booking a guided tour, or simply follow the signs and stop at any of the welcoming wineries along the way.

What to Do in the Prosecco Hills

Wine Tasting:
The main attraction here is, of course, the wine. Prosecco comes in several varieties—Brut, Extra Dry, Dry, and Cartizze, each with its own unique flavor profile. Most wineries offer tasting experiences where you can sample different types, often paired with local cheeses and cured

meats. It's a great way to learn about the region's history and winemaking traditions.

Visit a Local Osteria:
Stop by a traditional osteria (tavern) for a meal that pairs perfectly with Prosecco. Try soppressa, a local cured meat, or risotto al Prosecco, a creamy dish made with the sparkling wine you're here to taste. The food is simple but packed with flavor, reflecting the region's agricultural roots.

Explore the Vineyards by Bike:
For a more active way to explore, rent a bike and cycle through the vineyards. The paths are well-marked, and you'll pass through beautiful landscapes filled with grapevines, wildflowers, and small farmhouses. It's a peaceful way to take in the sights and enjoy the fresh air of the countryside.

Best Time to Visit

The Prosecco Hills are beautiful year-round, but here's what each season offers:

- **Spring (March-May):** The vineyards come alive with fresh green leaves and blooming wildflowers. It's a lovely time for cycling and outdoor wine tastings.
- **Summer (June-August):** Warm weather and sunny skies make it perfect for sipping chilled Prosecco outdoors. It's

busier during the summer, so book your winery tours in advance.
- **Fall (September-November):** Harvest season is the best time to visit. The vineyards are filled with workers picking grapes, and many wineries offer special harvest events and tastings. The autumn colors are spectacular, too.
- **Winter (December-February):** The hills are quieter, and there's a cozy, festive atmosphere in the villages. It's a great time for a more intimate wine tasting experience.

Where to Stay

There are plenty of charming places to stay in the Prosecco Hills:

- **Luxury:** Stay at Relais Duca di Dolle, a stunning agriturismo with beautiful rooms and a vineyard view.
- **Mid-Range:** Villa Abbazia in Follina offers a cozy atmosphere and great proximity to local wineries.
- **Budget:** For a more affordable option, try La Vigna di Sarah, a welcoming B&B surrounded by vineyards.

C. The Charming Lakeside Town of Bellagio

Welcome to Bellagio, often called the "Pearl of Lake Como." If you're dreaming of a picture-perfect Italian village where cobblestone streets wind between pastel-colored buildings and the sparkling waters of Lake Como are just a step away, then Bellagio is your ideal destination. This lakeside gem is filled with charm, elegance, and breathtaking views that will make you feel like you've stepped into a storybook. Let's explore Bellagio together and uncover why it's one of the most beloved spots in Northern Italy.

Where You Are: The Heart of Lake Como

You're in Bellagio, a small town that sits at the tip of the peninsula where Lake Como's three branches meet. The location offers spectacular views of the lake, surrounded by the lush foothills of the Alps. Bellagio is known for its elegant villas, vibrant gardens, and relaxed yet sophisticated atmosphere. Whether you're here for a romantic getaway, a nature-filled adventure, or just to soak up the scenery, Bellagio is the perfect place to slow down and savor the beauty of Northern Italy.

Must-See Sights

1. Villa Melzi Gardens:
One of the most beautiful spots in Bellagio is the Villa Melzi Gardens, a lakeside oasis filled

with exotic plants, ancient sculptures, and colorful flowers. As you stroll along the shaded pathways, you'll be treated to panoramic views of Lake Como. The gardens are the perfect place for a quiet walk or a picnic by the water, surrounded by the scent of blooming camellias and azaleas. Don't miss the small chapel and the charming pond filled with water lilies—it's a peaceful retreat that feels worlds away from the hustle and bustle.

2. Bellagio's Historic Center:
The heart of Bellagio is a delightful maze of narrow, cobblestone streets lined with boutique shops, cafés, and gelaterias. Take your time exploring the Salita Serbelloni, a famous stepped street filled with artisanal shops selling silk scarves, leather goods, and handmade jewelry. Grab a gelato and find a spot to sit and people-watch—you'll get a real feel for the local life. The town's historic charm is evident in every corner, from the quaint piazzas to the stone buildings covered in ivy.

3. Punta Spartivento:
For the best view of Lake Como, head to Punta Spartivento, a scenic lookout point at the tip of the Bellagio peninsula. From here, you can see the three branches of the lake coming together, framed by the mountains in the distance. It's a magical spot, especially at sunset when the sky and water light up in shades of pink and gold.

Bring your camera—this is one of the most photographed spots in Bellagio.

What to Do in Bellagio

Bellagio may be a small town, but there's plenty to do to fill your days. Rent a boat for a few hours and explore the lake at your own pace, stopping at nearby villages like Varenna and Menaggio. The waters are calm and perfect for a leisurely cruise. If you prefer to stay on land, take a hiking trail up into the hills behind Bellagio for stunning views of the lake and the surrounding countryside.

For a more relaxing experience, book a wine tasting at a local enoteca (wine bar). Bellagio is known for its Prosecco and other wines from the Lombardy region. Sip a glass of bubbly while enjoying a cheese platter filled with local specialties like Taleggio and Gorgonzola.

Where to Stay

Bellagio offers a range of accommodations, from luxurious lakeside hotels to charming bed and breakfasts:

- **Luxury**: Stay at the iconic Grand Hotel Villa Serbelloni, a 5-star hotel with opulent rooms, a private beach, and spectacular views of the lake.

- **Mid-Range**: Check out Hotel Du Lac, right in the heart of Bellagio, offering comfortable rooms and a rooftop terrace with panoramic views.
- **Budget**: For a more affordable stay, try Hotel Il Perlo Panorama, a cozy family-run hotel with stunning views of Lake Como from every room.

Best Time to Visit

Bellagio is beautiful year-round, but here's what each season brings:

- **Spring (March-May):** The gardens are in full bloom, and the weather is perfect for outdoor activities. It's a quieter time to visit before the summer crowds arrive.
- **Summer (June-August):** The peak season, with warm weather and plenty of tourists. It's the best time for swimming, boating, and dining outdoors by the lake.
- **Fall (September-November):** The crowds thin out, and the autumn colors make the landscape even more stunning. It's also a great time for wine tastings and enjoying local food festivals.
- **Winter (December-February):** Bellagio is quieter and feels cozier during the winter months. While some attractions may be closed, it's a peaceful time to visit and enjoy the holiday lights and decorations.

D. The Unseen Beauty of Friuli Venezia Giulia

Welcome to Friuli Venezia Giulia, a hidden gem of Northern Italy that many travelers overlook. This diverse region is like a beautiful secret waiting to be discovered, offering everything from snow-capped mountains and serene lakes to charming villages and pristine beaches along the Adriatic coast. Friuli Venezia Giulia is a place where cultures collide—you'll find Italian, Austrian, and Slovenian influences in everything from the architecture to the food. If you're searching for an off-the-beaten-path experience, you've come to the right place. Let's uncover the magic of this lesser-known region together!

Where You Are: Italy's Northeastern Treasure

You're in Friuli Venezia Giulia, tucked away in Italy's northeastern corner, bordered by Austria, Slovenia, and the Adriatic Sea. This region is a mix of landscapes—alpine peaks in the north, rolling vineyards in the center, and sandy beaches to the south. It's a melting pot of cultures and languages, with Italian, German, and Slovenian all commonly spoken. Here, you can explore medieval castles, sample world-class wines, and relax in picturesque seaside towns, all in one trip.

Must-See Sights

1. Trieste: The City of Coffee and Culture

Start your journey in Trieste, a vibrant city that feels more Central European than Italian. Trieste is famous for its historic cafés, like Caffè San Marco, where writers like James Joyce once sipped their espresso. Stroll along the Piazza Unità d'Italia, the largest sea-facing square in Europe, and take in the stunning views of the Adriatic Sea. Don't miss the Castello di Miramare, a beautiful white castle perched on the edge of the sea, surrounded by lush gardens.

2. Cividale del Friuli: A Step Back in Time

Head to Cividale del Friuli, a charming town with deep historical roots. It was founded by Julius Caesar and is now a UNESCO World Heritage Site. Visit the Tempietto Longobardo, an ancient Lombard temple with intricate carvings, and cross the Devil's Bridge for a stunning view of the emerald-green Natisone River. The town is a peaceful place to wander, with cobblestone streets, quaint shops, and plenty of spots to enjoy a glass of local wine.

3. The Collio Wine Region: A Taste of Friuli

Wine lovers, this one's for you. The Collio region is famous for its white wines, especially the crisp Friulano and Sauvignon Blanc. Take a scenic drive through the rolling hills dotted with vineyards, and stop at a few family-run wineries for tastings. Many of the wineries offer tours that include tastings of their best wines paired with local cheeses and cured meats. It's the perfect way to experience the flavors of the region and meet the winemakers who keep these traditions alive.

What to Do in Friuli Venezia Giulia

Hike the Julian Alps:
If you love the great outdoors, the Julian Alps in the northern part of the region are a must-visit. There are countless trails that offer spectacular views of the peaks and valleys. For a breathtaking experience, head to Lago di Fusine, a stunning glacial lake with crystal-clear waters reflecting the surrounding mountains. It's a fantastic spot for hiking, picnicking, or simply relaxing by the water.

Explore the Coastal Town of Grado:
Known as the "Sunny Island," Grado is a charming seaside town with sandy beaches, narrow streets, and a laid-back vibe. It's the perfect place to unwind after exploring the mountains and vineyards. Enjoy a walk along the waterfront promenade, visit the ancient Basilica of Santa Eufemia, and try the local seafood specialties at a seaside restaurant.

Taste the Local Cuisine:
Friuli Venezia Giulia's food scene is a blend of Italian, Austrian, and Slovenian influences, making it unlike any other region in Italy. Don't miss frico, a crispy cheese pancake made with local Montasio cheese, or goulash, a hearty stew

that reflects the region's Austro-Hungarian heritage. For dessert, try gubana, a sweet pastry filled with nuts, raisins, and chocolate.

Best Time to Visit

Friuli Venezia Giulia is a year-round destination, but here's what each season offers:

- **Spring (March-May):** The countryside is lush and green, and it's a great time for hiking and exploring the vineyards. The weather is mild, and wildflowers are in full bloom.
- **Summer (June-August):** The beaches of Grado and Lignano Sabbiadoro are bustling with activity, and it's the best time for enjoying the coast. It's also peak season for wine festivals and outdoor events.
- **Fall (September-November):** The vineyards turn golden, and it's the perfect time for wine tasting and enjoying harvest season. The weather is cooler, and the autumn colors make the landscape even more stunning.
- **Winter (December-February):** The mountains are covered in snow, making it a great time for skiing and snowshoeing in the Julian Alps. Trieste's cafés are cozy spots to warm up with a hot chocolate or espresso.

Where to Stay

Friuli Venezia Giulia has a range of accommodations, from luxury hotels to charming agriturismos:

- **Luxury:** Stay at Grand Hotel Duchi d'Aosta in Trieste for an elegant experience with a touch of old-world charm.
- **Mid-Range:** Agriturismo La Subida near Cormons offers cozy rooms and an incredible on-site restaurant serving regional specialties.
- **Budget:** For an affordable stay, try Ostello Tergeste in Trieste, a welcoming hostel with sea views.

E. Modena

If you're ready to dive deep into Italian culture and savor the true taste of Northern Italy, welcome to Modena! This charming city in the heart of the Emilia-Romagna region is best known for its world-famous balsamic vinegar, but trust me, Modena has so much more to offer. From its historic streets and elegant piazzas to a rich culinary tradition that goes far beyond vinegar, Modena is a place where food, art, and passion come together beautifully. Let's explore Modena together and uncover the hidden treasures that make this city a must-visit destination.

Where You Are: A Culinary Capital in Emilia-Romagna

You've arrived in Modena, a city that's all about tradition and flavor. It's located right in the middle of the Emilia-Romagna region, known as Italy's food valley. The city is famous for its aceto balsamico tradizionale di Modena (traditional balsamic vinegar), luxury cars like Ferrari and Maserati, and its vibrant cultural scene. Modena is a place where history meets innovation, making it perfect for those who want to experience authentic Italian life away from the bigger tourist crowds.

Must-See Sights

1. The Modena Cathedral (Duomo di Modena):
Start your exploration at the Duomo di Modena, a UNESCO World Heritage Site and one of the finest examples of Romanesque architecture in Italy. The cathedral's stunning marble façade and intricate sculptures tell stories of ancient legends. Step inside to admire the impressive vaulted ceilings and beautiful carvings. Don't miss the Ghirlandina Tower, the city's iconic bell tower—climb to the top for panoramic views of Modena's red rooftops and surrounding countryside.

2. Mercato Albinelli:

Foodies, this one's for you. Mercato Albinelli is Modena's bustling food market, filled with stalls selling fresh produce, cured meats, cheeses, and, of course, balsamic vinegar. It's a feast for the senses—take your time wandering through the aisles, sampling local specialties, and chatting with the friendly vendors. Grab a slice of prosciutto di Modena or some Parmigiano-Reggiano, and enjoy a taste of the region's best.

3. Casa Museo Luciano Pavarotti:
Modena is the birthplace of Luciano Pavarotti, one of the greatest opera singers of all time. Visit the Casa Museo Pavarotti, his former home turned museum, to learn about his life and legacy. You'll get a peek into his personal world, with memorabilia, costumes, and recordings that highlight his incredible career. It's a must-visit for music lovers and offers a unique glimpse into Modena's cultural heritage.

What to Eat and Drink in Modena

Let's get to the heart of Modena—its food. The city's culinary scene is legendary, and it's not just about balsamic vinegar (though you'll definitely want to try some). Start your meal with gnocco fritto, a fried dough served with cured meats like culatello and salame di Felino. Next, indulge in tortellini in brodo, delicate pasta parcels filled with meat and served in a rich, savory broth—it's a classic Modenese dish that feels like a warm hug.

And then, there's the balsamic vinegar. Make sure you try aceto balsamico tradizionale di Modena, aged for at least 12 years and drizzled over everything from grilled meats to fresh strawberries. It's thick, sweet, and full of complex flavors that will leave you wanting more.

To drink, try a glass of Lambrusco, Modena's signature sparkling red wine. It's light, fruity, and pairs perfectly with the hearty local dishes. Finish your meal with a sip of nocino, a walnut liqueur that's a local favorite.

Best Time to Visit

Modena is a wonderful place to visit any time of year, but here's what each season offers:

- **Spring (March-May):** The weather is mild, and the city's parks and gardens are in full bloom. It's a great time for strolling through the historic center and enjoying outdoor cafés.
- **Summer (June-August):** The city can get warm, but it's also when Modena's food and wine festivals are in full swing. Visit early in the morning or later in the evening to avoid the midday heat.
- **Fall (September-November):** This is harvest season, making it the best time

for food lovers. The markets are overflowing with fresh produce, and the local restaurants offer seasonal dishes featuring truffles and mushrooms.
- **Winter (December-February):** Modena feels cozy and festive in the winter, with holiday lights and traditional Christmas markets. It's the perfect time to enjoy a steaming bowl of tortellini in brodo.

Where to Stay

Modena has plenty of options for every type of traveler:

- **Luxury:** Stay at Hotel Rua Frati 48 in San Francesco, a beautifully restored historic building with elegant rooms and top-notch service.
- **Mid-Range:** Hotel Cervetta 5 offers a stylish, comfortable stay right in the heart of the city.
- **Budget:** For a more affordable option, try Ostello San Filippo Neri, a welcoming hostel with a great location and friendly atmosphere.

F. Parma

If you're craving a true taste of Italy, welcome to Parma—the land of prosciutto, Parmigiano-Reggiano, and some of the finest food in the world. This charming city in the heart of the Emilia-Romagna region is a paradise for food lovers and anyone looking to experience authentic Italian culture. Parma's appeal goes far beyond its delicious cuisine; it's a city filled with history, beautiful architecture, and a lively local atmosphere. Let's dive into Parma together and uncover what makes this place a hidden gem in Northern Italy.

Where You Are: The Culinary Heart of Emilia-Romagna

You've arrived in Parma, a city that's synonymous with exceptional food and quality ingredients. It's located in the Po Valley, one of Italy's most fertile agricultural areas, where the finest products are made using traditional methods passed down through generations. Parma is also a UNESCO Creative City for Gastronomy, recognized for its outstanding culinary heritage. Beyond the food, Parma is known for its elegant architecture, vibrant music scene (it's the birthplace of Giuseppe Verdi), and a welcoming spirit that makes you feel right at home.

Must-See Sights

1. Parma Cathedral (Duomo di Parma):
Start your visit at the Duomo di Parma, a stunning Romanesque cathedral famous for its frescoes by Correggio, including the breathtaking Assumption of the Virgin on the

dome. The interior is filled with beautiful sculptures and artworks that will leave you in awe. Next door, visit the Baptistery of Parma, with its pink marble exterior and fascinating medieval frescoes inside.

2. Teatro Regio di Parma:
Parma is a city of music, and the Teatro Regio is a must-visit for any opera lover. This historic theater is one of Italy's most prestigious opera houses and hosts performances by world-renowned artists. If you're visiting during the annual Verdi Festival in October, you're in for a treat—the whole city comes alive with music, celebrating the legacy of Giuseppe Verdi.

3. Palazzo della Pilotta:
Explore the Palazzo della Pilotta, a grand complex that houses several important museums, including the National Gallery (Galleria Nazionale) and the Teatro Farnese, a stunning wooden theater built in the 17th century. It's a fascinating place to learn about Parma's rich history and art, with works by Italian masters like Leonardo da Vinci and Titian.

What to Eat and Drink in Parma

The food in Parma is legendary, and no visit here would be complete without indulging in the city's most iconic dishes. Start your culinary adventure with Prosciutto di Parma, the world-famous dry-cured ham that's sweet, delicate, and melts in your mouth. It's best enjoyed simply—thinly sliced and paired with a glass of local wine.

Next, try Parmigiano-Reggiano, the "King of Cheese." Parma is one of the few places where this delicious, nutty cheese is produced. Visit a local cheese factory to see how it's made and enjoy a tasting session. The cheese is aged for at least 24 months, developing a complex flavor that's perfect on its own or grated over pasta.

For a hearty meal, order tortelli d'erbetta, a traditional pasta filled with ricotta cheese and spinach, served with melted butter and Parmesan. And don't leave Parma without trying a slice of Torta Duchessa, a rich dessert made with chocolate and amaretti cookies.

To drink, savor a glass of Lambrusco, a sparkling red wine that pairs perfectly with the local meats and cheeses. It's light, refreshing, and the perfect complement to Parma's rich flavors.

Best Time to Visit

Parma is delightful year-round, but here's what you can expect during each season:

- **Spring (March-May):** The weather is mild, and the countryside is in full bloom. It's a great time for exploring the markets and enjoying outdoor dining.

- **Summer (June-August):** The city can get warm, but it's also when food festivals are in full swing. It's the best time to experience Parma's vibrant nightlife and outdoor events.
- **Fall (September-November):** This is harvest season, making it the ideal time for food lovers. The local markets are overflowing with fresh produce, and it's the perfect time for wine and cheese tastings.
- **Winter (December-February):** Parma feels cozy and festive in winter, with Christmas markets and seasonal specialties like cotechino (a traditional sausage) served with lentils.

Where to Stay

Whether you're looking for luxury or a cozy local experience, Parma has something for everyone:

- **Luxury:** Stay at the elegant Grand Hotel de la Ville, offering stylish rooms and a central location near the best sights.
- **Mid-Range:** Hotel Button is a charming, family-run hotel that offers comfortable rooms and a friendly atmosphere in the heart of Parma's historic center.
- **Budget:** For an affordable stay, check out Parma Hostel, a welcoming place with clean rooms and great access to public transport.

Chapter 5: Itinerary Planning

A. 7-Day Highlights Itinerary

Day 1: Arrive in Venice

Your journey begins in the enchanting city of Venice. After checking into your hotel, start by exploring St. Mark's Square (Piazza San Marco). Visit the stunning St. Mark's Basilica with its golden mosaics, and the majestic Doge's Palace. Wander along the Grand Canal and enjoy a classic gondola ride through Venice's narrow canals. In the evening, indulge in a Venetian dinner with seafood risotto or bigoli pasta.

- **Overnight**: Venice

Day 2: Venice's Islands – Murano, Burano, and Torcello

Dedicate your second day to exploring the picturesque islands of the Venetian Lagoon. Begin with Murano, famous for its glass-making studios, where you can watch artisans create beautiful glass pieces. Head to Burano, a colorful fishing village known for its lace-making and vibrant houses. Wrap up with a visit to Torcello, one of the oldest settlements in the lagoon, and take in its ancient cathedral. Return to Venice in the evening.

- **Overnight**: Venice

Day 3: Verona

In the morning, travel to Verona, just an hour by train from Venice. Start with a visit to Juliet's House, where you can see the famous balcony and leave a note on the wall for luck in love. Then, explore Piazza delle Erbe, a lively square filled with markets, and admire the ancient Verona Arena, a Roman amphitheater still used for concerts. Enjoy a romantic dinner in a cozy trattoria.

- **Overnight**: Verona

Day 4: Lake Como

Next, make your way to the stunning Lake Como. Begin in Bellagio, the "Pearl of Lake Como," where you can stroll through its charming streets and admire the views of the lake and mountains. Take a boat ride to visit Varenna and Menaggio, two other picturesque towns along the shore. In Bellagio, treat yourself to a lakeside dinner and soak in the serene atmosphere as the sun sets.

- **Overnight**: Lake Como

Day 5: Milan

Spend day five exploring Milan, Italy's fashion and business capital. Start at the iconic Duomo di Milano and climb to the rooftop for panoramic views of the city. Then, visit Galleria Vittorio Emanuele II, Italy's oldest shopping mall, filled with luxury shops and historic cafés. Make a stop at Leonardo da Vinci's Last Supper (be sure to book tickets in advance). End the day with an aperitivo in the lively Navigli district.

- **Overnight**: Milan

Day 6: Modena

Today, take a short trip to Modena, a city renowned for its balsamic vinegar and culinary delights. Start with a visit to a traditional balsamic vinegar producer, where you can taste the rich, aged vinegar and learn about the process. Next, explore Modena Cathedral and Piazza Grande, both UNESCO World Heritage Sites. If you're a car enthusiast, don't miss the

Ferrari Museum nearby. Enjoy a meal of local tortellini and Prosciutto di Modena.

- **Overnight**: Bologna or Modena

Day 7: Bologna

Wrap up your trip in Bologna, the culinary capital of Northern Italy. Wander through Piazza Maggiore and marvel at the Basilica di San Petronio. Climb the Torre degli Asinelli for a final breathtaking view of the city. Don't leave Bologna without trying tagliatelle al ragù (Bolognese sauce) and other local favorites at Mercato di Mezzo. Spend the afternoon exploring the city's porticos and shopping for culinary souvenirs before catching your evening flight home.

- **Overnight**: Bologna (or catch a late evening flight)

B. 10-Day Comprehensive Itinerary

Day 1: Arrive in Venice

Start your journey in Venice, a city unlike any other. After settling into your hotel, explore St. Mark's Square, visiting St. Mark's Basilica and the Doge's Palace. Take a classic gondola ride through Venice's quiet canals, and end the day with a seafood dinner in the Cannaregio district, where the locals dine.

- **Overnight**: Venice

Day 2: Venice's Surrounding Islands

Take a ferry to explore the islands of the Venetian Lagoon. Start with Murano for its famous glass-making studios, then head to Burano with its vibrant houses and lace-making tradition, and wrap up in Torcello, one of Venice's oldest settlements. Return to Venice for a sunset along the Grand Canal.

- **Overnight**: Venice

Day 3: Verona

Travel to Verona by train (about an hour from Venice). Visit Juliet's House and the famous balcony, explore Piazza delle Erbe, and marvel at the Verona Arena, a Roman amphitheater still in use for performances. Enjoy dinner in a charming trattoria and try local dishes like risotto all'Amarone.

- **Overnight**: Verona

Day 4: Lake Garda

From Verona, take a short train or bus ride to Lake Garda, Italy's largest lake. Start in Sirmione, a beautiful lakeside town with a historic castle and thermal baths. Wander the charming streets, take a dip in the lake, and enjoy a leisurely lakeside lunch. Head to Malcesine for a scenic cable car ride up Monte Baldo for stunning lake views.

- **Overnight**: Verona

Day 5: Dolomites

Leave Verona early and head north to the Dolomites, one of Italy's most breathtaking natural regions. Settle into a village like Cortina d'Ampezzo or Ortisei. Spend the day hiking, exploring trails with panoramic mountain views, or simply relaxing in an alpine setting. Take in the fresh mountain air and end the day with a hearty dinner at a local alpine restaurant.

- **Overnight**: Dolomites

Day 6: Lake Como

Travel to Lake Como and arrive in Bellagio. Spend the day wandering through Bellagio's narrow, cobblestone streets, enjoying the scenic views of the lake and Alps. Take a boat tour to nearby towns like Varenna and Menaggio for a more complete experience of Lake Como's charm. Dine lakeside and soak in the serene beauty of the area.

- **Overnight**: Lake Como

Day 7: Milan

Head to Milan for a day filled with art, history, and style. Start at the Duomo di Milano, climbing to the rooftop for sweeping views. Visit Leonardo da Vinci's Last Supper (book tickets in advance) and explore Galleria Vittorio Emanuele II for a mix of luxury shopping and Italian café culture. In the evening, enjoy an aperitivo in the Navigli district.

- **Overnight**: Milan

Day 8: Prosecco Hills

From Milan, make your way to the Prosecco Hills between Conegliano and Valdobbiadene. Spend the day touring vineyards, tasting sparkling Prosecco, and enjoying the rolling hills. Visit small family-run wineries and sample wines paired with local cheeses and meats. Relax with a scenic drive or a quiet picnic among the vineyards.

- **Overnight**: Prosecco Hills

Day 9: Modena

Head south to Modena, a city known for its culinary heritage. Start your day with a tour of a balsamic vinegar producer to sample the rich, aged vinegar Modena is famous for. Visit the Modena Cathedral and Piazza Grande, both UNESCO World Heritage Sites. If you're a car enthusiast, stop by the Ferrari Museum. End your day with a traditional meal, featuring tortellini and Prosciutto di Modena.

- **Overnight**: Modena

Day 10: Bologna

Spend your final day in Bologna, a city with one of Italy's most celebrated food scenes. Explore Piazza Maggiore and the Basilica di San Petronio, then stroll under Bologna's famous porticos. Don't miss the Mercato di Mezzo food market, where you can sample local delicacies like tagliatelle al ragù and fresh mortadella. Wrap up with a final meal at a local osteria before catching your evening train or flight.

- **Overnight**: Bologna (or departure)

C. 14-Day In-Depth Itinerary

Days 1-2: Venice

Begin your journey in Venice. Spend your first day exploring St. Mark's Basilica and Doge's Palace in St. Mark's Square, then enjoy a gondola ride through the narrow canals. On day two, venture to the islands of Murano (famous for glassmaking), Burano (with its colorful houses and lace-making tradition), and Torcello (known for its ancient cathedral). Return to Venice for a scenic dinner by the canal.

- **Overnight**: Venice

Days 3-4: Verona and Lake Garda

Travel to Verona, home of Shakespeare's Romeo and Juliet. Visit Juliet's House, Piazza delle Erbe, and the Verona Arena. On day four, take a short trip to Lake Garda, where you can explore Sirmione with its medieval castle, and Malcesine, where a cable car ride up Monte Baldo offers spectacular views. Enjoy lakeside dining with views of the serene waters.

- **Overnight**: Verona

Days 5-6: Dolomites

From Verona, head to the Dolomites and settle into a village like Cortina d'Ampezzo or Ortisei. Spend these two days hiking through scenic trails like Tre Cime di Lavaredo and exploring the charming alpine villages. Don't miss Lago di Braies, a stunning turquoise lake surrounded by towering peaks. In the evening, relax with a meal of local alpine cuisine.

- **Overnight**: Dolomites

Days 7-8: Lake Como

Travel to Lake Como and check into Bellagio or Varenna. Spend your first day exploring Bellagio's elegant gardens and cobblestone streets, then take a boat ride around the lake, visiting Menaggio and Tremezzo. On day eight, relax by the lake or take a private boat tour for an up-close look at the luxury villas that dot the shoreline.

- **Overnight**: Lake Como

Day 9: Milan

Head to Milan for a day of history, art, and style. Visit the Duomo di Milano and climb to its rooftop, then see Leonardo da Vinci's Last Supper (reserve tickets in advance). Stroll through Galleria Vittorio Emanuele II for some shopping or an espresso at an iconic café. End the day in the vibrant Navigli district for an aperitivo by the canals.

- **Overnight**: Milan

Days 10-11: Prosecco Hills

From Milan, travel to the Prosecco Hills between Conegliano and Valdobbiadene. Spend your days visiting family-run wineries, tasting sparkling Prosecco, and enjoying the scenic rolling vineyards. Drive along the Prosecco Wine Road and stop at small towns for authentic Italian meals. Take a relaxing walk through the vineyards, or enjoy a peaceful picnic with local delicacies.

- **Overnight**: Prosecco Hills

Days 12-13: Modena and Parma

Travel south to Modena, known for its balsamic vinegar and motor heritage. Start with a visit to a traditional balsamic vinegar producer, then explore the Modena Cathedral and Piazza Grande. On day thirteen, visit nearby Parma, where you can taste Prosciutto di Parma and Parmigiano-Reggiano at local producers. Discover Parma's Cathedral and the Baptistery, and end the day with a meal of tortelli d'erbetta in a local trattoria.

- **Overnight**: Modena or Parma

Day 14: Bologna

End your trip in Bologna, Italy's food capital. Explore Piazza Maggiore and the Basilica di San Petronio, then stroll through Bologna's iconic porticos. Visit Mercato di Mezzo for local delights like tagliatelle al ragù and fresh mortadella. Take a moment to climb the Torre degli Asinelli for a final panoramic view of this beautiful city before departing for home.

- **Overnight**: Bologna (or departure)

Chapter 6: Cultural Experiences

A. Must-Visit Museums and Art Galleries

Hello there, culture enthusiast!

If you're excited about art, history, and discovering the stories behind Italy's masterpieces, you're in for a treat. Let's explore some of the must-visit museums and galleries that will leave you inspired and amazed.

1. The Uffizi Gallery (Florence)

The Uffizi Gallery is one of the most famous art museums in the world and a must-visit for anyone traveling through Florence. Housed in a historic building along the Arno River, this gallery showcases masterpieces from the Italian Renaissance. Here, you can marvel at Botticelli's The Birth of Venus, Leonardo da Vinci's Annunciation, and Michelangelo's Doni Tondo.

The museum's vast collection also includes works by Titian, Raphael, and Caravaggio. To avoid long lines, be sure to book your tickets in advance. Give yourself plenty of time to explore—you could easily spend hours getting lost in the beauty of these iconic paintings.

2. The Pinacoteca di Brera (Milan)

Located in the heart of Milan's bohemian Brera district, the Pinacoteca di Brera is a treasure trove of Italian art. It's home to an impressive collection of Renaissance and Baroque masterpieces, including The Marriage of the Virgin by Raphael and The Dead Christ by Mantegna. The gallery also features works by Caravaggio and Titian, making it a must-visit for art history buffs. After your visit, take a stroll through the surrounding neighborhood, filled with quaint cafés and boutique shops. The Brera district itself feels like an open-air museum, with its charming, artistic vibe.

3. The Egyptian Museum (Museo Egizio) (Turin)

For something different, head to Turin to visit the Egyptian Museum, the second-largest museum dedicated to Egyptian antiquities in the world (after Cairo). It's a fascinating journey back in time, with thousands of artifacts, including mummies, sarcophagi, and ancient statues. The museum offers a unique glimpse into the life and beliefs of ancient Egyptians, making it a must-see for history lovers. The collection is beautifully curated, with interactive displays and guided tours available in English.

4. The Accademia Gallery (Galleria dell'Accademia) (Florence)

If you're in Florence, don't miss the chance to see Michelangelo's David at the Accademia Gallery. This iconic statue is one of the most famous sculptures in the world, and seeing it up close is a truly awe-inspiring experience. The gallery also features other works by Michelangelo, as well as a collection of Renaissance paintings. It's a smaller museum, but the highlight—David—is worth the visit alone.

5. The Peggy Guggenheim Collection (Venice)

For a modern twist, visit the Peggy Guggenheim Collection in Venice, one of the most important museums of modern art in Italy. Housed in Peggy Guggenheim's former home along the Grand Canal, this gallery features works by Picasso, Pollock, Dalí, and Kandinsky. The museum's tranquil sculpture garden is the perfect place to relax after exploring the collection. It's a refreshing change of pace from the traditional Renaissance art you'll find elsewhere in Italy.

B. Historic Sites and Architectural Wonders

1. The Duomo di Milano (Milan)

The Duomo di Milano is one of Italy's most iconic landmarks and a masterpiece of Gothic architecture. Known for its stunning marble façade and intricate details, this cathedral took nearly six centuries to complete. Climb to the rooftop to enjoy breathtaking views of Milan, where you can admire the intricate spires and statues up close. The Duomo is also home to countless artworks and religious relics, including the nail believed to be from Christ's crucifixion. It's a must-see destination that beautifully captures the spirit and artistry of Milan.

2. Arena di Verona (Verona)

One of the best-preserved Roman amphitheaters in the world, the Arena di Verona dates back to the 1st century AD. This grand structure once hosted gladiatorial contests and now serves as a magnificent open-air opera house. Attending a performance here is a truly unique experience, but even a daytime visit allows you to marvel at the arena's ancient stonework and remarkable acoustics. Located in the heart of Verona, it's a reminder of the city's rich Roman heritage and an essential stop for any history lover.

3. The Leaning Tower of Pisa (Pisa)

Although not technically in Northern Italy, the Leaning Tower of Pisa is close enough that many travelers include it in their itineraries. This iconic architectural wonder is famous for its unintended tilt, caused by soft ground that couldn't fully support the structure's weight. Visitors can climb the tower's spiral staircase for panoramic views of Pisa. The tower, along with the nearby Pisa Cathedral and Baptistery in the Piazza dei Miracoli, offers a striking example of Romanesque architecture and is a UNESCO World Heritage site.

4. Basilica di San Vitale (Ravenna)

Ravenna's Basilica di San Vitale is a hidden gem and one of the most important examples of Byzantine art and architecture in Western Europe. Built in the 6th century, the basilica is famous for its spectacular mosaics that cover the walls and ceilings, depicting intricate biblical scenes and figures. The vibrant colors and detailed artistry transport you to another era, reflecting the religious and cultural influences of the Byzantine Empire. It's a truly awe-inspiring site and a must-visit for anyone interested in medieval history and art.

5. Castello Sforzesco (Milan)

Originally built in the 15th century, Castello Sforzesco is a grand fortress that showcases Milan's powerful past. This castle was once home to the ruling Sforza family and has been transformed over the centuries into a beautiful complex that houses several museums. Inside, you'll find a collection of Renaissance art, including Michelangelo's unfinished Rondanini Pietà. The castle's gardens and courtyards are free to explore and offer a peaceful escape within the bustling city.

6. St. Mark's Basilica (Venice)

No visit to Venice would be complete without seeing St. Mark's Basilica. Known for its blend of Byzantine, Gothic, and Renaissance architecture, this basilica is an architectural marvel with its golden mosaics, domes, and intricate marble details. Built in the 9th century, it was originally intended to house the remains of St. Mark, Venice's patron saint. Take time to admire the shimmering mosaics, the beautiful Pala d'Oro (Golden Altar), and the view of Piazza San Marco from the basilica's balcony.

C. Local Festivals and Events You Can't Miss

1. Venice Carnival (Carnevale di Venezia)

- **When**: February (dates vary each year)
- **Where**: Venice

The Venice Carnival is one of the most iconic and spectacular events in Italy. For two weeks, the city transforms into a theatrical stage filled with lavish costumes, ornate masks, and grand parades. The celebration dates back to the 12th century and was originally a time for Venetians to indulge before Lent. Today, it's a dazzling display of creativity and tradition. Be sure to attend the Flight of the Angel, where a performer gracefully "flies" from the bell tower of St. Mark's Basilica. Don't forget to don a mask and join in the festivities—it's a magical experience that will transport you back in time.

- **Tip**: Book your accommodation early, as Venice gets very crowded during Carnival. If you want an authentic experience, consider attending one of the exclusive masquerade balls held in historic palaces.

2. Alba White Truffle Fair (Fiera Internazionale del Tartufo Bianco d'Alba)

- **When**: October to November
- **Where**: Alba, Piedmont

If you're a food lover, the Alba White Truffle Fair is a must-visit. Held in the charming town of Alba, this festival celebrates the white truffle, one of the most prized delicacies in Italian cuisine. During the fair, the entire town is filled with the intoxicating aroma of truffles, and you can sample truffle-infused dishes at local restaurants and food stalls. The highlight is the truffle auction, where top-quality truffles are sold to the highest bidder. There are also cooking demonstrations, wine tastings, and a bustling truffle market where you can buy fresh truffles to take home.

Tip: Pair your truffle tasting with a glass of local Barolo or Barbaresco wine—it's the perfect complement to the earthy, aromatic flavor of the truffles.

3. Opera Festival at the Arena di Verona

- **When:** June to September
- **Where:** Verona

The Opera Festival at the Arena di Verona is a truly unique experience. Held in a magnificent Roman amphitheater that dates back to the 1st century, this festival features world-class opera performances under the stars. The arena's incredible acoustics make it the perfect venue for iconic operas like Aida, La Traviata, and Carmen. The festival attracts opera enthusiasts from all over the world, but you don't have to be an opera expert to enjoy it—just sitting in the historic arena, surrounded by the grandeur of ancient Rome, is an unforgettable experience.

- **Tip:** Arrive early and bring a cushion, as the stone seats can be hard. For a more comfortable experience, consider booking a seat in the reserved section.

4. The Palio di Siena

- **When**: July 2 and August 16
- **Where**: Siena (Tuscany)

While technically in Central Italy, the Palio di Siena is close enough to be a popular day trip for those exploring Northern Italy. This historic horse race dates back to the Middle Ages and is held in the heart of Siena's Piazza del Campo. The race is fast and intense, with riders representing different city districts (contrade) competing for glory. It's more than just a race—it's a display of deep-rooted tradition, with elaborate parades, colorful costumes, and intense rivalries. The atmosphere is electric, and the whole city comes alive with excitement.

- **Tip**: If you want a good view of the race, consider purchasing a ticket for a seat in the stands or arriving early to find a spot in the center of the piazza.

5. Battle of the Oranges (Ivrea Carnival)

- **When**: February (dates vary each year)
- **Where**: Ivrea, Piedmont

The Battle of the Oranges is one of the most unique and lively festivals in Italy. It's part of the Ivrea Carnival, where the townspeople reenact a historic rebellion by throwing oranges at each other. The battle represents the citizens' fight against tyranny, and participants are divided into teams—those on foot (representing the townspeople) and those in carts (representing the tyrant's army). It's a chaotic, colorful event filled with flying oranges, laughter, and lots of fun.

- **Tip**: Wear old clothes or rent protective gear (including a red hat) if you plan to participate. Spectators can enjoy the action from the sidelines but should be prepared for some flying fruit!

Chapter 7: The Culinary Delights of Northern Italy

A. Traditional Dishes You Must Try

1. Risotto alla Milanese (Lombardy)

Starting in Milan, Risotto alla Milanese is a classic dish you won't want to miss. This creamy risotto is infused with saffron, which gives it its distinct golden color and a subtly earthy flavor. It's typically prepared with carnaroli rice, which is known for its ability to absorb flavors while maintaining a creamy texture. Often paired with ossobuco (braised veal shank), Risotto alla Milanese is rich, warming, and a true taste of Lombardian cuisine.

2. Tortellini in Brodo (Emilia-Romagna)

Emilia-Romagna is known as Italy's "food valley," and tortellini in brodo is one of its most beloved traditional dishes. Tortellini, tiny pasta filled with a mix of pork, prosciutto, and Parmesan, are served in a clear, flavorful broth. It's simple but deeply comforting, and you'll find it especially popular during the winter months. Locals often enjoy this dish as a holiday meal, making it perfect for those cold evenings in Bologna or Modena.

3. Bagna Cauda (Piedmont)

For something a bit different, try Bagna Cauda in Piedmont. This dish is like a warm, savory fondue made with garlic, anchovies, olive oil, and butter. It's served with an assortment of raw and cooked vegetables for dipping, such as bell peppers, cardoons, and celery. Traditionally, Bagna Cauda is a communal dish meant to be enjoyed with friends and family. It's rich, flavorful, and a perfect way to warm up after a day of exploring.

4. Pesto alla Genovese (Liguria)

When you think of Italian pesto, you're thinking of Pesto alla Genovese from Liguria. This fresh, vibrant sauce is made with basil, pine nuts, garlic, Parmesan, and olive oil. While it's often served with trofie or trenette pasta, pesto can also be used to flavor minestrone or spread on crusty bread. The delicate aroma and flavor of fresh basil make this dish an unforgettable taste of Liguria's coastline.

5. Vitello Tonnato (Piedmont)

Vitello Tonnato is a cold dish of thinly sliced veal served with a creamy, tuna-flavored sauce. This unusual combination of veal and tuna may sound surprising, but the flavors blend beautifully. It's typically garnished with capers and sometimes lemon zest, adding a bright note to the rich, smooth sauce. You'll find this dish in many restaurants around Turin, and it's especially popular as an antipasto (starter) in the summer months.

6. Casoncelli (Lombardy)

Casoncelli is a type of stuffed pasta native to Lombardy, particularly popular in the Bergamo and Brescia areas. These crescent-shaped pasta pockets are filled with a mix of beef, pork, breadcrumbs, and sometimes even a touch of fruit, like raisins or pears, which adds a hint of sweetness. They're typically served with browned butter, sage, and pancetta, creating a delicious blend of savory and sweet flavors.

7. Polenta e Funghi (Various Regions)

Polenta, a creamy dish made from cornmeal, is a staple across Northern Italy, often served as a base for other dishes. One of the most popular variations is Polenta e Funghi (polenta with mushrooms), where the creamy polenta is topped with a mix of sautéed wild mushrooms. You'll find this comforting dish especially popular in mountainous regions like Trentino and Veneto, where mushrooms are plentiful. It's a hearty, rustic dish that's perfect for a chilly evening.

8. Risi e Bisi (Veneto)

A dish that hails from the Veneto region, Risi e Bisi (rice and peas) is a Venetian classic that's somewhere between risotto and soup. Made with Vialone Nano rice and fresh spring peas, this dish is light yet comforting. It's traditionally eaten on April 25th, Venice's feast day for St. Mark, but you can find it served year-round. Topped with a sprinkle of Parmesan and a touch of fresh parsley, Risi e Bisi is a lovely example of simple, seasonal Italian cooking.

9. Brasato al Barolo (Piedmont)

A dish that's as rich in flavor as it is in heritage, Brasato al Barolo is a beef roast braised in Barolo wine, one of Italy's finest reds from Piedmont. The meat is slow-cooked with onions, carrots, and celery until it's tender and infused with the wine's complex flavors. This dish is typically served with polenta or mashed potatoes and is a fantastic choice for wine lovers who want to experience the deep flavors of Piedmontese cuisine.

10. Frittura di Pesce (Veneto)

For a taste of Northern Italy's seafood, try Frittura di Pesce along the coast, especially in Venice. This dish is a delightful mix of lightly fried fish, shrimp, and squid, often served with lemon wedges and a sprinkle of salt. It's a simple preparation, but the freshness of the seafood makes it extraordinary. It's perfect to enjoy on a sunny day by the water, paired with a crisp glass of local white wine.

B. Best Restaurants You Should Consider

To savor these traditional dishes, consider visiting the following renowned restaurants in Northern Italy:

1. Il Luogo di Aimo e Nadia (Milan, Lombardy): A two-Michelin-starred restaurant offering a refined take on traditional Lombard cuisine.

- **Address:** Via Privata Raimondo Montecuccoli, 6, 20147 Milan, Italy

- **Contact:** +39 02 416886

- **Features:** Elegant dining rooms, extensive wine list, and seasonal menus.

2. Osteria Francescana (Modena, Emilia-Romagna): Helmed by Chef Massimo Bottura, this three-Michelin-starred restaurant is celebrated for its innovative interpretations of traditional Italian dishes.

- **Address:** Via Stella, 22, 41121 Modena MO, Italy

- **Contact:** +39 059 223912

- **Features:** Contemporary art-filled interiors, tasting menus, and a focus on local ingredients.

3. Trattoria della Posta (Monforte d'Alba, Piedmont): A charming trattoria offering authentic Piedmontese dishes in a rustic setting.

- **Address:** Località Sant'Anna, 87, 12065 Monforte d'Alba CN, Italy

- **Contact:** +39 0173 78120

- **Features:** Cozy atmosphere, seasonal menus, and an extensive selection of local wines.

4. Antica Osteria del Bai (Genoa, Liguria): Overlooking the sea, this historic osteria specializes in Ligurian seafood dishes, including traditional pesto.

- **Address:** Via al Molo Giano, 16128 Genoa GE, Italy

- **Contact:** +39 010 246 4416

- **Features:** Seaside views, fresh seafood, and a selection of regional wines.

5. **Ristorante Al Covo (Venice, Veneto):** A family-run restaurant known for its dedication to traditional Venetian cuisine and fresh, locally sourced ingredients.

- **Address:** Campiello de la Pescaria, 3968, 30122 Venice VE, Italy

- **Contact:** +39 041 522 3812

- **Features:** Intimate setting, seasonal menus, and a focus on sustainable seafood.

C. Wine Regions and Tasting Tours

1. Piedmont

Piedmont, located in the foothills of the Alps, is home to some of Italy's most famous red wines, including Barolo and Barbaresco. Known as the "King of Wines," Barolo is made from the Nebbiolo grape and is celebrated for its bold flavors, rich tannins, and complex aromas of cherry, rose, and truffle. Barbaresco, a lighter but equally elegant wine, is also crafted from Nebbiolo and offers delicate floral notes.

Best Tasting Experience: Visit the Wine Museum at Barolo Castle, where you can learn about the history of winemaking in the region. Then, head to a family-owned winery like Gaja Winery in Barbaresco for a guided tasting tour.
- **Contact:** Gaja Winery, Via Torino 18, 12050 Barbaresco CN, Italy | +39 0173 635294
- **Tip:** Pair your tasting with local delicacies like tajarin pasta and truffle-infused dishes for a true Piedmont experience.

2. Veneto

Veneto is one of Italy's most prolific wine-producing regions, offering a wide range of styles from the light and bubbly Prosecco to the deep, rich Amarone della Valpolicella. Prosecco, made from the Glera grape, is perfect for those who love a refreshing sparkling wine, while Amarone is a bold, full-bodied red made using dried grapes, resulting in a wine with intense, concentrated flavors.

Best Tasting Experience: Explore the Prosecco Hills between Conegliano and Valdobbiadene. Visit a local vineyard like Nino Franco Winery for a Prosecco tasting, then head to Valpolicella for a

tour of Allegrini Estate, known for its exquisite Amarone wines.
- **Contact:** Nino Franco Winery, Via Garibaldi 147, 31049 Valdobbiadene TV, Italy | +39 0423 976975
- **Tip:** Try pairing Prosecco with seafood and light appetizers, while Amarone is best enjoyed with grilled meats or aged cheeses.

3. Trentino-Alto Adige

Trentino-Alto Adige is Italy's northernmost wine region, known for its cool-climate wines. The region produces aromatic whites like Gewürztraminer and Pinot Grigio, as well as elegant reds like Lagrein and Schiava. The alpine climate and high-altitude vineyards give these wines a crisp acidity and vibrant flavor, making them perfect for pairing with local mountain cuisine.

Best Tasting Experience: Visit the charming town of Bolzano, where you can tour wineries like Cantina Tramin, known for its outstanding Gewürztraminer. For a more immersive experience, take the South Tyrolean Wine Road, which winds through picturesque vineyards and offers numerous tasting stops.
- **Contact:** Cantina Tramin, Strada del Vino 144, 39040 Termeno BZ, Italy | +39 0471 096630

- **Tip:** Enjoy a glass of crisp Pinot Grigio with fresh alpine cheeses or local speck (cured ham).

4. Friuli Venezia Giulia

Friuli Venezia Giulia is a wine lover's dream, particularly for those who enjoy white wines. The region's cool climate and unique terroir make it perfect for growing Pinot Grigio, Friulano, and Sauvignon Blanc. Friuli's wines are known for their aromatic intensity and balanced acidity, offering a refreshing taste that pairs beautifully with seafood and light dishes.

Best Tasting Experience: Head to the Collio wine region, where you can visit wineries like Venica & Venica, a family-run estate known for its excellent white wines. Enjoy a guided tasting and stroll through the scenic vineyards.
- **Contact:** Venica & Venica, Località Cerò 8, 34071 Dolegna del Collio GO, Italy | +39 0481 61264
- **Tip:** Pair Friulano with fresh seafood dishes or a plate of local San Daniele prosciutto for a true taste of the region.

5. Lombardy

Lombardy offers a diverse wine scene, but it's best known for its sparkling Franciacorta and the robust red wines of Valtellina. Franciacorta is Italy's answer to Champagne, made using the traditional method with Chardonnay, Pinot Noir, and Pinot Blanc grapes. Valtellina, on the other hand, is famous for its Nebbiolo-based wines, which have a distinct minerality and elegance thanks to the region's steep, terraced vineyards.

Best Tasting Experience: Start with a tour of the Franciacorta Wine Route, visiting top producers like Ca' del Bosco, known for its exceptional sparkling wines. Then, head to the Valtellina region for a tasting at Nino Negri, one of the oldest and most respected wineries.
- **Contact:** Ca' del Bosco, Via Albano Zanella 13, 25030 Erbusco BS, Italy | +39 030 7766111
- **Tip**: Enjoy Franciacorta with a plate of antipasti, while Valtellina wines pair beautifully with hearty dishes like pizzoccheri (buckwheat pasta with cheese and potatoes).

Chapter 8: Outdoor Activities and Adventures

A. Hiking in the Italian Alps and Dolomites

If you're looking to experience the wild beauty of Northern Italy, then hiking in the Italian Alps and Dolomites should be at the top of your list. Whether you're a seasoned hiker or a beginner, there's something magical about exploring these towering giants on foot. So, lace up your hiking boots, grab your backpack, and let's set off on an unforgettable adventure!

Where You Are

You're in the heart of the Italian Alps and Dolomites, some of the most iconic mountain ranges in the world. The Dolomites, with their jagged limestone peaks, are a UNESCO World Heritage Site and famous for their dramatic landscapes. The Italian Alps, stretching across the northern border of Italy, offer equally stunning views and a range of hiking experiences, from gentle walks to challenging climbs. These mountains are not only about natural beauty—they're steeped in history and culture, with charming alpine villages dotting the landscape.

Must-Try Hiking Trails

1. Tre Cime di Lavaredo (Dolomites)

The Tre Cime di Lavaredo (Three Peaks of Lavaredo) is one of the most famous hikes in the Dolomites, and for good reason. The loop trail around these towering peaks offers incredible views at every turn. It's a moderate hike that takes about 4-5 hours to complete, making it perfect for a day trip. You'll walk through alpine meadows filled with wildflowers, pass by beautiful mountain lakes, and get up-close views of the iconic limestone peaks. Bring your camera—you'll want to capture the stunning scenery along the way.

- **Tip:** Start early to avoid crowds, especially in the summer. There are several mountain huts (rifugi) along the trail where you can stop for a meal or a drink. Don't miss the chance to try local dishes like polenta or apple strudel.

2. Sentiero del Viandante (Lake Como)

If you prefer a trail with a mix of mountain and lake views, head to the Sentiero del Viandante (Path of the Wayfarer) along Lake Como. This historic hiking route dates back to Roman times and offers stunning panoramas of the lake and surrounding mountains. The trail stretches for about 25 miles (40 km) and can be broken up into shorter sections if you're looking for a more relaxed hike. You'll pass through charming villages like Varenna and Bellano, where you can stop for a lakeside picnic or a refreshing gelato.

- **Tip:** Pack a swimsuit! Some sections of the trail have easy access to the lake, so you can take a quick dip to cool off before continuing your hike.

3. Alta Via 1 (Dolomites)

For the more experienced hiker, the Alta Via 1 is a must-do. Known as the "High Route," this multi-day trek takes you through the heart of the Dolomites, covering about 75 miles (120 km). The trail typically takes 7-10 days to complete and offers a challenging yet rewarding experience with views of jagged peaks, deep valleys, and picturesque mountain huts. Each night, you'll stay in a rifugio, where you can enjoy a hearty meal and a warm bed, making it a unique way to experience the mountains.

- **Tip**: Book your rifugio stays in advance, especially during the summer months. The trail is well-marked, but bring a good map and be prepared for changing weather conditions.

What to Pack for Your Hike

Packing for a hike in the Alps or Dolomites is all about being prepared. Here's a quick checklist to make sure you have everything you need:

- **Sturdy Hiking Boots:** The trails can be rocky and uneven, so a good pair of boots is essential.
- **Layers of Clothing:** The weather can change quickly in the mountains, so bring a mix of lightweight and warm layers, including a waterproof jacket.
- **Snacks and Water:** Even if you plan to stop at a rifugio, it's a good idea to carry some trail mix, energy bars, and plenty of water.
- **Sun Protection:** Bring a hat, sunglasses, and sunscreen—the sun can be intense at high altitudes.
- **Map and Navigation Tools:** While many trails are well-marked, it's always smart to carry a map or GPS device.

Best Time to Hike

The hiking season in the Italian Alps and Dolomites typically runs from late June to early October. In July and August, the weather is warm, and the trails are clear of snow, making it the best time for hiking. However, it's also the busiest season, so if you prefer a quieter experience, consider visiting in September when the crowds thin out, and the autumn colors start to appear.

- **Tip:** In June and early October, some higher-altitude trails may still have snow. Check local trail conditions before setting out.

B. Lake Activities: Sailing, Kayaking, and Swimming

1. Sailing on Lake Como

Lake Como is known for its elegance, luxury villas, and stunning scenery, making it one of the most iconic lakes in Northern Italy. But beyond its glamorous reputation, Lake Como is a fantastic spot for sailing. With consistent winds and calm waters, it's a dream for both novice and experienced sailors.

- **Where to Go:** The towns of Bellagio, Varenna, and Menaggio are great starting points for sailing tours. Many companies offer private or group sailing experiences,

allowing you to glide across the water and take in views of the majestic Alps.
- **What to Expect**: Picture yourself on a sleek sailboat, the wind in your hair, and the sun shining on the sparkling blue water. You'll pass by historic villas, charming villages, and lush gardens that line the lake's shores.
- **Tip**: If you're new to sailing, consider booking a guided tour with a local skipper who can show you the best spots and share stories about the lake's history and famous residents.

Contact for Sailing Tours:
- **Bellagio Sailing:** Via Valassina 73, 22021 Bellagio CO, Italy | +39 349 560 0603

2. Kayaking on Lake Garda

If you prefer a more active and immersive experience, kayaking on Lake Garda is an excellent choice. As Italy's largest lake, Garda offers diverse landscapes—from steep cliffs and rocky shores in the north to gentle beaches and olive groves in the south. Kayaking allows you to explore hidden coves, paddle close to the cliffs, and discover secluded beaches that you can't reach by foot.

- **Where to Go:** Start your kayaking adventure in towns like Riva del Garda or Malcesine, where the water is

crystal-clear, and the views are spectacular. Both locations offer rentals and guided tours for all skill levels.
- **What to Expect:** As you paddle along, you'll see dramatic cliffs, small islands, and even ancient ruins along the shoreline. It's a peaceful way to experience the lake, with the sound of your paddle dipping into the water and the occasional splash of fish jumping nearby.
- **Tip:** Rent a kayak early in the morning when the water is calmest. Be sure to bring a waterproof bag for your belongings and plenty of sunscreen—there's no shade out on the lake!

Contact for Kayak Rentals:
- **Garda Kayak Tours**: Piazzale Porto, 38066 Riva del Garda TN, Italy | +39 0464 554 444

3. Swimming in Lake Maggiore

If you're looking for a refreshing swim, head to Lake Maggiore, one of Italy's most beautiful lakes. Nestled between Italy and Switzerland, Lake Maggiore boasts crystal-clear waters and stunning mountain backdrops. The lake's mild climate makes it a popular swimming spot during the summer months, with plenty of designated beaches and swimming areas.

- **Where to Go:** Check out Lido di Cannero Riviera, a lovely beach area with soft sand, clear water, and facilities like showers, sunbeds, and a beach café. It's a family-friendly spot, perfect for a day of swimming and sunbathing.
- **What to Expect:** The water in Lake Maggiore is usually cool and refreshing, perfect for a hot summer day. You can swim out to floating platforms, dive off rocks, or simply float on your back and enjoy the views of the surrounding mountains.
- **Tip:** Pack a picnic and make a day of it. There are plenty of shaded spots along the shore where you can relax and enjoy a meal with a view of the lake.

Contact for Beach Info:
- **Lido di Cannero Riviera:** Via Massimo d'Azeglio, 28821 Cannero Riviera VB, Italy | +39 0323 788108

Best Time for Lake Activities

The best time to enjoy lake activities in Northern Italy is from late spring to early fall (May to September). During these months, the weather is warm, and the water is perfect for swimming and boating. July and August are the busiest months, so if you prefer a quieter experience, visit in June or September when the crowds are smaller, but the weather is still beautiful.

C. Winter Sports

1. Cortina d'Ampezzo

Known as the "Queen of the Dolomites," Cortina d'Ampezzo is one of the most prestigious ski resorts in Italy. It's part of the Dolomiti Superski area, offering access to over 745 miles (1,200 km) of interconnected slopes. Whether you're here for skiing, snowboarding, or just soaking up the beautiful scenery, Cortina d'Ampezzo has something for everyone.

- **What to Expect**: The resort features a mix of beginner, intermediate, and advanced runs, as well as snow parks for freestyle enthusiasts. The stunning Dolomite peaks provide a dramatic backdrop, making every run a scenic experience. Don't miss the famous Tofana di Rozes slope for breathtaking views.
- **Other Activities**: If you're not skiing, try snowshoeing or take a scenic ride on the cable car for a panoramic view of the surrounding mountains. Cortina also offers excellent après-ski options, with plenty of cozy bars and restaurants.
- **Contact**: Cortina Ski Resort Info: Via Marangoi, 1, 32043 Cortina d'Ampezzo BL, Italy | +39 0436 866252

2. Livigno:

Nestled near the Swiss border, Livigno is a winter sports haven known for its reliable snowfall and extensive ski terrain. The resort boasts over 70 miles (115 km) of slopes and is famous for its duty-free shopping, making it a favorite destination for those looking to combine skiing with some retail therapy.

- **What to Expect:** Livigno's ski area is divided into two main sections: Mottolino Fun Mountain and Carosello 3000. Mottolino is perfect for snowboarders and freestyle skiers, offering one of the best snow parks in Europe. Carosello 3000 features wide, sunny slopes that are ideal for families and beginner skiers.
- **Other Activities:** Aside from skiing and snowboarding, Livigno offers ice skating, snowmobiling, and cross-country skiing. After a day on the slopes, relax in the town's thermal spa or explore its lively nightlife scene.
- **Contact:** Livigno Ski Resort Info: Plaza Placheda, Via Saroch, 1098/A, 23030 Livigno SO, Italy | +39 0342 052200

3. Val Gardena

Val Gardena, located in the heart of the Dolomites, is part of the Dolomiti Superski network and is one of the most popular ski destinations in Northern Italy. It's known for its well-groomed slopes, stunning mountain scenery, and excellent infrastructure, making it a great choice for skiers and snowboarders of all levels.

- **What to Expect:** The Sella Ronda, a famous ski circuit, allows you to ski around the entire Sella mountain range in one day, covering over 25 miles (40 km) of slopes. Val Gardena also has a variety of terrain parks, perfect for freestyle skiing and snowboarding.
- **Other Activities:** If you need a break from the slopes, try tobogganing or explore the charming alpine villages of Ortisei, Santa Cristina, and Selva di Val Gardena. You can also take a guided snowshoeing tour through the peaceful winter landscape.
- **Contact**: Val Gardena Tourist Info: Str. Meisules, 213, 39048 Selva di Val Gardena BZ, Italy | +39 0471 777777

4. Bormio

For a more relaxed and traditional Italian ski experience, head to Bormio. This historic spa town is known for its thermal baths and excellent ski slopes, making it the perfect place to combine winter sports with relaxation. Bormio offers a range of runs for all skill levels, and its high-altitude slopes ensure great snow conditions throughout the season.

- **What to Expect:** Bormio's ski area includes the famous Stelvio slope, one of the most challenging downhill runs in the world. The resort also has plenty of easier slopes, making it a great destination for families and beginner skiers.
- **Other Activities:** After a day on the slopes, unwind in Bormio's thermal baths, which have been used since Roman times. The town also has a charming historic center filled with quaint shops and restaurants.
- **Contact:** Bormio Ski Resort Info: Via Battaglion Morbegno, 25, 23032 Bormio SO, Italy | +39 0342 901451

Best Time for Winter Sports

The ski season in Northern Italy typically runs from December to April, with the best snow conditions in January and February. The Christmas holiday period can be busy, so if you prefer quieter slopes, plan your visit for late January or early March when the weather is still excellent, but the crowds have thinned out.

D. Biking Through Scenic Countryside Trails

1. The South Tyrol Wine Road (Strada del Vino) – Trentino-Alto Adige

Imagine biking through endless vineyards with the stunning backdrop of the Dolomite Mountains—that's what you'll find on the South Tyrol Wine Road. This 25-mile (40 km) trail winds through one of Italy's most beautiful wine regions, known for its crisp white wines like Pinot Grigio and Gewürztraminer. The route is mostly flat and paved, making it perfect for a leisurely ride.

What to Expect: You'll pedal past charming towns like Bolzano, Caldaro, and Termeno, each offering plenty of opportunities to stop and taste local wines. Along the way, you'll find quaint wine bars and cellars where you can take a break and enjoy a glass of the region's best.
- **Tip:** Plan your ride in late spring or early fall for the best weather and the chance to see the vineyards in full bloom or harvest. Consider renting an e-bike if you want to take it easy and still cover the entire trail.

Contact for Bike Rentals:
- **South Tyrol Bike Rental**: Via Dr. Joseph Streiter 1, 39100 Bolzano BZ, Italy | +39 0471 234567

2. The Mincio River Bike Path

The Mincio River Bike Path is a flat, family-friendly trail that stretches for about 28 miles (45 km), connecting the beautiful towns of

Peschiera del Garda on Lake Garda to Mantua in Lombardy. It's one of the most popular cycling routes in Northern Italy, known for its scenic views and peaceful atmosphere.

- **What to Expect:** Starting at Peschiera del Garda, you'll ride alongside the tranquil Mincio River, passing through fields of sunflowers, ancient fortresses, and lush countryside. The trail ends in the Renaissance city of Mantua, where you can explore historic palaces and piazzas.
- **Tip:** Stop at the village of Borghetto sul Mincio, famous for its watermills and picturesque views. It's a great spot for lunch, where you can try local specialties like tortellini di Valeggio.

Contact for Bike Rentals:
- **Peschiera Bike Rental**: Via Venezia 24, 37019 Peschiera del Garda VR, Italy | +39 045 7550101

3. The Valtellina Trail

For those seeking a more adventurous ride, the Valtellina Trail offers an unforgettable experience in the heart of the Italian Alps. This 70-mile (110 km) trail follows the Adda River through the Valtellina Valley, known for its stunning mountain views, terraced vineyards, and historic villages.

- **What to Expect:** The trail takes you through charming towns like Tirano and Sondrio, offering plenty of spots to stop and taste local wines like Sforzato and Valtellina Superiore. The route is mostly flat with a few gentle climbs, making it suitable for moderate cyclists.
- **Tip**: Visit in the summer when the weather is warm and the valley is lush and green. Don't miss the chance to stop at a local trattoria for a meal of pizzoccheri, a hearty buckwheat pasta dish typical of the region.

Contact for Bike Rentals:
- **Valtellina Bike Tours**: Piazza Cavour 3, 23037 Tirano SO, Italy | +39 0342 701418

4. The Dolomites Cycling Route

The Dolomites Cycling Route is perfect for experienced cyclists looking for a challenge. This trail winds through the heart of the Dolomites, offering steep climbs, thrilling descents, and spectacular mountain views. It's a part of the famous Sella Ronda circuit, which can be completed in a day by seasoned riders.

- **What to Expect:** The route covers about 34 miles (55 km) and takes you through iconic mountain passes like Passo Sella, Passo Gardena, and Passo Pordoi. The climbs are challenging, but the views from

the top are worth every pedal stroke. You'll see jagged peaks, lush valleys, and charming alpine villages along the way.
- **Tip**: If you're not up for the full ride, consider joining a guided e-bike tour, which makes the climbs more manageable. Bring plenty of water and snacks—the high-altitude air can be dehydrating.

Contact for Bike Rentals:
- **Dolomiti Bike Rental**: Via Dolomiti 7, 32020 Arabba BL, Italy | +39 0436 79128

Best Time for Biking in Northern Italy

The best time to explore these trails is from May to October, when the weather is warm and the paths are clear of snow. July and August are the busiest months, so if you prefer a quieter experience, plan your ride for June or September. The autumn season also offers beautiful fall foliage, especially in the vineyard regions.

Chapter 9: Shopping in Northern Italy

A. Luxury Shopping in Milan

If you're dreaming of luxury boutiques, designer labels, and stylish streets, then Milan is your ultimate shopping destination in Northern Italy. Let's explore the best spots for luxury shopping and make sure you don't miss a single stylish find.

1. Via Montenapoleone

Welcome to Via Montenapoleone, the crown jewel of Milan's Quadrilatero della Moda (Fashion District). This iconic street is home to some of the world's most prestigious fashion houses and luxury brands, including Gucci, Prada, Versace, and Armani. If you're looking for the latest in haute couture, this is the place to be.

- **What to Expect:** As you stroll down Via Montenapoleone, you'll be surrounded by elegant storefronts displaying everything from bespoke suits and stunning evening gowns to the latest handbags and shoes. Even if you're just window-shopping, it's a fantastic place to soak in the sophisticated Milanese vibe and spot the latest trends.
- **Tip:** Don't hesitate to step inside the boutiques, even if you're not planning to make a purchase. The staff are used to welcoming fashion lovers from all over the world, and you might just find a hidden gem or get inspired by the latest collections.
- **Address:** Via Montenapoleone, 20121 Milan, Italy
- **Contact for Information:** +39 02 7740 4343

2. Galleria Vittorio Emanuele II

The Galleria Vittorio Emanuele II is more than just a shopping mall—it's a historic monument and one of the most beautiful places to shop in Milan. Built in the 19th century, this stunning glass-roofed arcade is often called the "living room of Milan." It's home to luxury stores like Louis Vuitton, Prada, and Dolce & Gabbana, as well as high-end cafés and restaurants.

- **What to Expect:** The Galleria's elegant design, with its iron and glass dome and mosaic floors, creates a shopping experience like no other. Take your time browsing the designer boutiques, and be sure to stop at the Prada flagship store, one of the oldest in the city. When you need a break, enjoy an espresso at Camparino in Galleria, a historic café that has been serving patrons since 1915.
- **Tip:** Don't forget to spin on your heel on the mosaic of the bull in the center of the Galleria. It's a tradition believed to bring good luck!

- **Address:** Piazza del Duomo, 20123 Milan, Italy
- **Contact for Information:** +39 02 8646 0000

3. La Rinascente

If you prefer everything in one place, head to La Rinascente, Milan's premier luxury department store located right next to the Duomo di Milano. This multi-level store features a curated selection of high-end fashion, accessories, cosmetics, and home goods from both Italian and international designers.

- **What to Expect:** La Rinascente offers a mix of top designer labels like Fendi,

Balenciaga, and Valentino, as well as up-and-coming brands. The ground floor is dedicated to beauty and accessories, while the upper floors showcase women's and men's fashion. Don't miss the food hall on the top floor, where you can find gourmet Italian products and enjoy a meal with a spectacular view of the Duomo's spires.
- **Tip:** If you're looking for unique Italian souvenirs, check out the store's selection of fine Italian leather goods, artisanal jewelry, and specialty foods.

- **Address:** Piazza del Duomo, 20121 Milan, Italy
- **Contact for Information:** +39 02 88521

4. The Armani Megastore

No trip to Milan would be complete without visiting the Armani Megastore, a flagship location for one of Italy's most iconic fashion brands. Spread across multiple floors, this store offers everything from Giorgio Armani's high-fashion collections to the more casual Emporio Armani line. You'll also find a selection of accessories, fragrances, and home decor items.

- **What to Expect:** The Armani Megastore is a sleek, modern space designed to reflect the brand's minimalist aesthetic. It's not

just a place to shop—it's an experience, complete with the elegant Emporio Armani Caffè where you can enjoy a coffee or aperitivo.
- **Tip:** Check out the Armani Casa section for stylish home decor items. It's a great place to pick up unique, high-quality gifts.

- **Address:** Via Alessandro Manzoni, 31, 20121 Milan, Italy
- **Contact for Information:** +39 02 7231 8444

5. Corso Vittorio Emanuele II

If you're looking for a blend of luxury and more accessible fashion, head to Corso Vittorio Emanuele II, one of Milan's main shopping streets. Here, you'll find high-end boutiques alongside popular high-street brands like Zara, H&M, and Uniqlo.

- **What to Expect:** The street is bustling with shoppers, street performers, and stylish locals. It's a great place to enjoy a leisurely stroll, browse the shops, and take in the vibrant atmosphere of Milan's fashion scene. Be sure to pop into the Mango flagship store for chic, affordable styles.
- **Tip:** Visit during Milan Fashion Week (held in February and September) for a chance to see the city at its most fashionable. You

might even catch a glimpse of a runway show or a celebrity sighting!

- **Address:** Corso Vittorio Emanuele II, 20122 Milan, Italy
- **Contact for Information:** +39 02 7740 4343

B. Local Markets and Artisan Shops

1. Mercato di Porta Palazzo (Turin, Piedmont)

Let's start in Turin, where the Mercato di Porta Palazzo offers a vibrant and lively shopping experience. Known as the largest open-air market in Europe, this market has been a staple in Turin for centuries. It's the perfect place to explore if you're looking for fresh produce, cheeses, meats, and even household goods.

- **What to Expect:** The market is divided into different sections, each offering a unique experience. You'll find fresh fruits and vegetables in one area, while another is dedicated to local delicacies like Toma cheese and Piedmontese meats. The indoor section features a variety of fresh fish and seafood. It's a sensory delight, with the smells of ripe tomatoes, fresh basil, and aged cheeses filling the air.
- **Tip:** Visit early in the morning when the market is most lively. Be sure to try some

bicerin, a traditional Turin drink made with coffee, chocolate, and cream, at a nearby café.

- **Location:** Piazza della Repubblica, 10122 Turin, Italy
- **Opening Hours:** Monday to Saturday, 7 AM – 2 PM
- **Contact:** +39 011 442 2001

2. Mercato di Rialto (Venice, Veneto)

In the heart of Venice, the Mercato di Rialto is a historic market located along the Grand Canal, just steps away from the famous Rialto Bridge. This market has been operating for over 1,000 years, and it's still a vital part of daily life in Venice.

- **What to Expect:** The Rialto Market is famous for its fresh seafood, brought in daily by local fishermen. You'll find everything from squid and octopus to clams and Venetian lagoon fish. The produce section is just as impressive, filled with seasonal fruits, vegetables, and herbs. It's a fantastic place to experience the local food culture and pick up fresh ingredients if you're staying in an apartment and plan to cook.
- **Tip:** The market is busiest early in the morning, so get there by 8 AM to see the best selection of fresh fish. Don't forget to

stop by a nearby bar for a cicchetti (Venetian tapas) and a glass of Prosecco.

- **Location:** Campo della Pescheria, 30125 Venice, Italy
- **Opening Hours:** Tuesday to Saturday, 7 AM – 12 PM
- **Contact:** +39 041 274 7981

3. Mercato Centrale (Florence, Tuscany)

While not technically in Northern Italy, Florence's Mercato Centrale is a must-visit if you're exploring the broader region. This indoor market is a foodie's paradise, offering an incredible selection of local Tuscan products, artisan foods, and handmade crafts.

- **What to Expect:** The ground floor is filled with stalls selling fresh meats, cheeses, breads, and olive oils. Upstairs, you'll find a bustling food court with a variety of vendors serving everything from fresh pasta to gourmet paninis. It's a great spot to sample local specialties like porchetta (roast pork) and ribollita (Tuscan soup).
- **Tip:** Bring an appetite and try a bit of everything. The upstairs food court is perfect for a quick and delicious lunch. Don't forget to pick up a bottle of Tuscan extra virgin olive oil to take home.

- **Location:** Piazza del Mercato Centrale, 50123 Florence, Italy
- **Opening Hours:** Daily, 8 AM – Midnight
- **Contact:** +39 055 239 9798

4. Artisan Shops in Bellagio (Lake Como, Lombardy)

The charming town of Bellagio on Lake Como is known for its boutique artisan shops. Here, you'll find a wide array of handcrafted goods, from silk scarves to hand-painted ceramics. It's the perfect place to find a unique souvenir or gift that reflects the elegance and beauty of the region.

- **What to Expect:** Bellagio's artisan shops are small and intimate, often run by local artists who have perfected their craft over generations. One of the most popular items to buy here is Como silk, known for its high quality and beautiful designs. You'll also find stunning pottery, leather goods, and jewelry.
- **Tip:** Take your time browsing the shops along Via Giuseppe Garibaldi. Stop by Azalea Silks for some of the finest silk scarves, ties, and accessories made from locally sourced silk.

- **Location:** Via Giuseppe Garibaldi, 22021 Bellagio CO, Italy

Contact: Azalea Silks, +39 031 951555

5. Mercato dell'Antiquariato (Milan, Lombardy)

If you love antiques and vintage items, don't miss the Mercato dell'Antiquariato along Milan's Navigli canals. Held on the last Sunday of each month, this antique market is one of the largest in Italy, attracting collectors and curious shoppers alike.

- **What to Expect:** The market features over 400 stalls selling a wide variety of antiques, including vintage jewelry, old books, furniture, and unique decorative pieces. It's a great place to find one-of-a-kind treasures and enjoy the lively atmosphere along the canals.
- **Tip:** Arrive early for the best selection, and be ready to haggle a bit—negotiating prices is part of the fun. After shopping, grab a coffee or aperitivo at one of the nearby canal-side cafés.
- **Location:** Alzaia Naviglio Grande, 20144 Milan, Italy
- **Opening Hours:** Last Sunday of the month, 8 AM – 6 PM
- **Contact:** +39 02 8940 9240

Tips for Shopping at Local Markets

- **Bring Cash:** While some stalls accept credit cards, many prefer cash, so it's a good idea to have euros on hand.
- **Ask About the Products:** Don't hesitate to chat with the vendors. They often have great stories about their products and love to share tips on how to use or prepare them.
- **Try Before You Buy:** At food markets, many vendors offer samples. It's a fantastic way to taste local flavors and discover new favorites.

C. What to Buy

When it comes to bringing home a piece of Northern Italy, you're in luck—this region is filled with unique, high-quality items that make perfect souvenirs. Let's explore the must-buy souvenirs and local products that you won't want to leave behind.

1. Italian Wines: Barolo, Prosecco, and Amarone

Wine lovers, rejoice! Northern Italy is home to some of the world's most famous wine regions, making it the perfect place to pick up a bottle (or two) as a souvenir. Here are the top picks:

- **Barolo (Piedmont):** Known as the "King of Wines," Barolo is a full-bodied red made from the Nebbiolo grape. It's celebrated for its bold tannins, complex flavors, and

long aging potential. It's a fantastic choice for collectors or anyone who loves robust red wines.
- **Prosecco (Veneto):** If you prefer something bubbly, grab a bottle of Prosecco from the Veneto region. It's light, refreshing, and perfect for celebrations. Look for bottles labeled "DOCG" for the highest quality.
- **Amarone della Valpolicella (Veneto):** For a unique red wine, try Amarone. It's made using dried grapes, which concentrate the flavors, resulting in a rich, velvety wine with notes of cherry, chocolate, and spice.

Tip: Most wineries offer shipping options, so you don't have to worry about carrying heavy bottles home. For a tasting experience, visit local enotecas (wine shops) where you can sample before buying.

2. Parmigiano-Reggiano and Prosciutto di Parma (Emilia-Romagna)

If you're a fan of Italian cuisine, you can't leave without some Parmigiano-Reggiano (Parmesan cheese) and Prosciutto di Parma (Parma ham). Both products are native to the Emilia-Romagna region and are protected by strict quality standards, ensuring you're getting the real deal.

- **Parmigiano-Reggiano:** Known as the "King of Cheeses," Parmesan is aged for at

least 24 months, developing a rich, nutty flavor. It's perfect for grating over pasta, enjoying with a glass of wine, or giving as a gift to a foodie friend.
- **Prosciutto di Parma:** This dry-cured ham is sweet, tender, and melts in your mouth. It's often sliced paper-thin and enjoyed as an antipasto with melon or cheese.

Tip: Buy these products vacuum-sealed from a reputable market or specialty shop. They'll last longer and be easier to transport. Look for the official PDO (Protected Designation of Origin) label to ensure authenticity.

3. Murano Glass from Venice

For a stunning, handcrafted souvenir, consider picking up a piece of Murano glass. Made on the island of Murano near Venice, these glass pieces are crafted using centuries-old techniques and come in a variety of styles, from colorful vases and sculptures to delicate jewelry.

- **What to Buy:** Popular items include glass pendants, chandeliers, and decorative figurines. Each piece is unique, showcasing the vibrant colors and intricate patterns that Murano glass is famous for.

Tip: Be sure to buy from an authorized dealer or directly from a glass-blowing studio on Murano Island to avoid counterfeit pieces. Authentic

Murano glass usually comes with a certificate of authenticity.

Where to Shop:
Venini Glass Factory, Fondamenta dei Vetrai 50, Murano, Italy | +39 041 273 7201

4. Italian Leather Goods from Florence and Milan

Northern Italy is known for its high-quality leather products, particularly in cities like Florence and Milan. Whether you're looking for a stylish handbag, a classic belt, or a sleek pair of shoes, you'll find beautiful, well-crafted leather goods that make perfect souvenirs.

- **What to Buy:** Leather jackets, wallets, handbags, and shoes are among the most popular items. Look for soft, supple leather with impeccable stitching—these are signs of high-quality craftsmanship.

Tip: Bargaining is common at local markets like Florence's San Lorenzo Market, but be respectful and polite. For designer pieces, visit upscale boutiques in Milan's fashion district.

Where to Shop:
The Bridge, Via della Spiga 23, Milan, Italy | +39 02 7600 2345

5. Silk from Lake Como

Lake Como isn't just known for its stunning scenery—it's also famous for producing some of the finest silk in the world. The tradition of silk weaving here dates back to the 16th century, and today, Como remains a hub for high-quality silk products.

- **What to Buy:** Look for silk scarves, ties, and pocket squares. They're lightweight, easy to pack, and make elegant gifts. You can also find silk fabrics and home decor items like cushions and curtains.

Tip: Visit the Silk Museum in Como to learn about the history of silk production and see the intricate weaving process up close.

Where to Shop:
Ratti Silk Shop, Via Regina 34, Como, Italy | +39 031 338 511

6. Hand-Painted Ceramics from Liguria

The region of Liguria, particularly towns like Albisola, is known for its beautiful hand-painted ceramics. These pieces are often decorated with vibrant colors and intricate designs, inspired by the sea and local flora.

- **What to Buy:** Plates, bowls, and vases are popular items. Each piece is unique, making it a special memento of your time in Italy.

Tip: Be sure to ask if the ceramics are dishwasher-safe, especially if you plan to use them regularly.

Where to Shop:
Ceramiche San Giorgio, Via Cristoforo Colombo 75, Albisola, Italy | +39 019 485 231

Tips for Buying Souvenirs in Northern Italy

- **Check for Authenticity:** Look for official labels like PDO, DOCG, or certificates of authenticity when buying specialty food products, wines, or artisanal crafts.
- **Pack Wisely:** Wrap fragile items in clothing or purchase protective packaging. Most shops offer shipping options if you're worried about carrying delicate items home.
- **Embrace Local Flavors:** Food products like olive oil, truffle oil, balsamic vinegar, and regional wines make excellent gifts. They're a delicious way to share your travel experience with friends and family back home.

Chapter 10: Accommodation Guide

A. Top Hotels, Boutique Stays, and Budget Options

Finding the perfect place to stay is a key part of making your trip to Northern Italy unforgettable. Let's explore some of the best places to lay your head after a day of exploring the beautiful cities, lakes, and countryside of Northern Italy.

1. Luxury Hotels

If you're looking to treat yourself to a bit of luxury, Northern Italy is home to some of Europe's most glamorous hotels. Here are the top picks for those who want to experience world-class service and stunning surroundings.

- **Hotel Principe di Savoia (Milan, Lombardy):** A true icon of Milan, this five-star hotel combines classic Italian elegance with modern comforts. The rooms are beautifully decorated, featuring marble bathrooms and plush furnishings. The hotel's spa is a perfect retreat after a day of shopping in the city's fashion district.

- **Address**: Piazza della Repubblica 17, 20124 Milan, Italy
- **Contact:** +39 02 62301
- **Price Range:** From $600 per night
- **Features**: Rooftop pool, luxury spa, fine dining restaurant

Grand Hotel Tremezzo (Lake Como, Lombardy): Overlooking the sparkling waters of Lake Como, this historic hotel is the epitome of luxury. With its art nouveau style, three swimming pools, and private beach, it's the perfect place for a romantic getaway or a relaxing escape.

- **Address**: Via Regina 8, 22016 Tremezzo CO, Italy
- **Contact**: +39 0344 42491
- **Price Range:** From $800 per night
- **Features**: Lakefront views, luxury spa, boat rentals

2. Boutique Stays

If you prefer smaller, more intimate accommodations with a personal touch,

Northern Italy's boutique hotels offer a charming alternative to larger chains. These properties often feature unique decor, friendly service, and a cozy atmosphere that makes you feel right at home.

Corte di Gabriela (Venice, Veneto): Tucked away in the heart of Venice, this boutique hotel is a hidden gem. The rooms are modern yet retain the charm of a Venetian palazzo, with exposed beams and stylish furnishings. The breakfast, served in a tranquil courtyard, is a highlight of any stay.

- **Address:** Calle Avvocati 3836, 30124 Venice, Italy
- **Contact:** +39 041 523 5077
- **Price Range:** From $300 per night
- **Features:** Central location, eco-friendly design, personalized service

Ostello Bello Grande (Milan, Lombardy): If you're seeking a hip, social vibe with boutique charm, this stylish hostel in Milan is a fantastic choice. It's perfect for younger travelers or those who want a budget-friendly stay without sacrificing style.

- **Address:** Via Lepetit 33, 20124 Milan, Italy
- **Contact:** +39 02 670 5921
- **Price Range:** From $100 per night for a private room

- **Features**: Rooftop terrace, free breakfast, social events

3. Budget Options

Traveling on a budget doesn't mean you have to compromise on comfort. Northern Italy offers plenty of wallet-friendly accommodations that provide clean, comfortable rooms and excellent service at affordable prices.

Hotel Berna (Milan, Lombardy): Located just steps from Milan's Central Station, Hotel Berna is a great choice for budget-conscious travelers who want a convenient and comfortable place to stay. The rooms are modern, and the staff goes above and beyond to make guests feel welcome.

- **Address**: Via Napo Torriani 18, 20124 Milan, Italy
- **Contact:** +39 02 679 5181
- **Price Range:** From $150 per night
- **Features:** Complimentary breakfast, free Wi-Fi, 24-hour front desk

Generator Venice (Venice, Veneto): This stylish hostel offers a mix of private rooms and dorms, making it a great option for both solo travelers and groups. Located on the island of Giudecca, it offers stunning views of Venice and a lively social scene.

- **Address:** Fondamenta Zitelle 86, Giudecca, 30133 Venice, Italy
- **Contact:** +39 041 877 8288
- **Price Range:** From $30 per night for a dorm bed, $100 for a private room
- **Features:** On-site bar, communal lounge, events and tours

B. Eco-Friendly and Unique Accommodation Choices

1. Eremito Hotelito del Alma (Umbria)

For a peaceful retreat in a truly unique setting, head to Eremito Hotelito del Alma. Nestled in the lush Umbrian countryside, this eco-friendly hotel is designed like a monastic retreat, offering a digital detox experience. The rooms, or "celluzze," are simple yet beautifully crafted, inspired by ancient monasteries.

- **What to Expect:** The hotel focuses on sustainability with solar energy, organic meals, and no Wi-Fi or television to encourage guests to disconnect. It's an ideal place for meditation, yoga, and enjoying the serene natural surroundings.
- **Tip:** Participate in the communal dinners, where guests share a vegetarian meal in a candlelit dining room—it's a highlight of the experience.

- **Address:** Località Tarina, 05010 Parrano TR, Italy
- **Contact:** +39 0763 891010
- **Price Range:** From $350 per night

2. La Bandita Townhouse (Pienza, Tuscany)

Located in the heart of the UNESCO-listed town of Pienza, La Bandita Townhouse is a boutique hotel that combines eco-friendly practices with modern luxury. The hotel was transformed from an old convent, preserving its historical charm while incorporating sustainable features.

- **What to Expect:** Expect solar panels, energy-efficient lighting, and a commitment to using locally sourced, organic products. The hotel's restaurant serves farm-to-table meals, highlighting the best of Tuscan cuisine with ingredients from nearby farms.
- **Tip:** Take advantage of the complimentary bikes to explore the charming town of Pienza and its stunning countryside.
- **Address:** Corso Il Rossellino, 111, 53026 Pienza SI, Italy
- **Contact:** +39 0578 749005
- **Price Range:** From $250 per night

3. Adler Lodge Ritten (South Tyrol)

If you're dreaming of a luxurious alpine escape with a focus on sustainability, Adler Lodge Ritten is the perfect choice. Situated in the Dolomites, this eco-friendly lodge features stunning views, a wellness spa, and a commitment to green practices.

- **What to Expect:** The lodge is powered by renewable energy and built using sustainable materials. The rooms are cozy and modern, with large windows that offer panoramic views of the mountains. Enjoy the farm-to-table dining experience, with fresh, organic ingredients sourced from local farms.
- **Tip:** Don't miss the guided nature walks offered by the lodge—they're a great way to learn about the local flora and fauna.
- **Address:** Via Maria Assunta 27, 39054 Soprabolzano, Italy
- **Contact:** +39 0471 1551 800
- **Price Range:** From $500 per night

4. **Locanda La Raia (Gavi, Piedmont)**

Located in the rolling hills of the Gavi wine region, Locanda La Raia is a stunning eco-friendly boutique hotel set on a biodynamic farm and winery. It's the perfect destination for wine lovers and those looking to reconnect with nature.

- **What to Expect**: The hotel is part of a sustainable estate that produces organic wines, honey, and vegetables. The rooms are elegantly decorated with natural materials, and guests can enjoy wine tastings, farm tours, and yoga classes. The on-site restaurant serves organic, seasonal dishes paired with the estate's wines.
- **Tip:** Book a wine tasting tour to sample their exceptional Gavi wines and learn about the biodynamic farming methods used on the estate.
- **Address:** Strada Monterotondo 79, 15066 Gavi AL, Italy
- **Contact:** +39 0143 642860
- **Price Range:** From $350 per night

5. Eco-Hotel Saltus (South Tyrol)

For an immersive nature experience, stay at Eco-Hotel Saltus, an eco-friendly hotel nestled in the forests of South Tyrol. Built with a focus on sustainability, the hotel offers a peaceful escape with stunning views of the surrounding mountains.

- **What to Expect:** The hotel's architecture blends seamlessly with the natural environment, using local wood and stone. It's heated by renewable energy and features a green rooftop. Guests can relax

in the forest sauna, enjoy yoga sessions, or take guided hikes through the nearby nature reserve.
- **Tip:** Try the hotel's vegetarian tasting menu, which showcases local, organic ingredients and offers a unique culinary experience.

- **Address:** Via Ibsen 17, 39050 San Genesio, Italy
- **Contact:** +39 0471 354134
- **Price Range:** From $300 per night

Tips for Choosing Eco-Friendly Accommodations

- **Look for Green Certifications:** Many eco-friendly hotels have certifications like the Green Key or LEED. These labels indicate a commitment to sustainable practices.
- **Support Local Businesses:** Staying at locally-owned boutique hotels or family-run guesthouses often means your money is going directly back into the community.
- **Ask About Green Practices:** Don't hesitate to ask the hotel about their sustainability efforts. Most eco-friendly accommodations are proud of their practices and happy to share details with guests.

190

Chapter 11: Practical Information

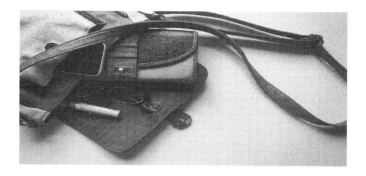

A. Emergency Contacts and Safety Tips for Travelers

1. Emergency Phone Numbers in Italy

Here's a quick list of the main emergency contacts you'll need while traveling in Northern Italy. These numbers work throughout the country and are free to call from any phone.

General Emergency (Ambulance, Fire, and Police): 112
This is the European emergency number, similar to 911 in the U.S. It connects you to a central dispatch operator who can direct your call to the appropriate service, whether you need police, an ambulance, or the fire department.
Medical Emergency (Ambulance): 118

For urgent medical assistance, call 118. The operators are trained to handle emergency situations and can provide guidance in English if necessary.
Police (Carabinieri): 112
For reporting crimes or suspicious activity, contact the Carabinieri, Italy's national police force.
Fire Department: 115
If you encounter a fire or need rescue services, dial 115.

- **Tip:** Save these numbers in your phone contacts as "Italian Emergency Numbers" before your trip so they're easily accessible in case of an emergency.

2. Local Emergency Contacts for Major Cities

If you're spending time in larger cities like Milan, Venice, or Florence, it's helpful to know the contact information for local tourist police and emergency services.

Milan Tourist Police: +39 02 7727 0000
Located near the Duomo, the tourist police can assist with lost property, theft reports, and general safety concerns.
Venice Tourist Assistance: +39 041 274 7070
Venice has a special police service for tourists, offering assistance with theft, lost passports, and other issues.

Florence Medical Assistance (Santa Maria Nuova Hospital): +39 055 27581
If you need urgent medical care in Florence, head to the Santa Maria Nuova Hospital, known for its English-speaking staff.

3. Safety Tips for Travelers in Northern Italy

While Northern Italy is generally very safe for travelers, it's always good to be aware of potential risks and take basic precautions to ensure a smooth trip.

- **Be Mindful of Pickpockets:** In crowded areas like train stations, markets, and popular tourist attractions, pickpocketing can be an issue. Keep your belongings secure, wear a crossbody bag, and avoid carrying valuables in your back pockets.
- **Use Reputable Transportation:** When taking taxis, use official taxi services rather than accepting rides from unmarked vehicles. For ride-sharing, apps like Uber are available in some cities, but it's best to use local taxi apps like FreeNow for safer options.
- **Stay Aware of Your Surroundings:** If you're exploring busy places like Milan's fashion district or Venice's Rialto Bridge, be alert and keep an eye on your belongings. Scams targeting tourists can occur, such as overly friendly strangers

offering unsolicited help or fake charity collectors.
- **Emergency Cash and Copies:** It's smart to keep a small amount of emergency cash separate from your main wallet, as well as copies of important documents like your passport, travel insurance, and credit cards.

Tip: If you lose your passport, contact your country's nearest consulate or embassy immediately for assistance in getting a replacement.

4. Travel Insurance

Having travel insurance is one of the best ways to protect yourself while exploring Northern Italy. A good travel insurance plan will cover unexpected events like medical emergencies, trip cancellations, lost luggage, or theft.

- **Medical Coverage:** Make sure your travel insurance includes medical coverage, as healthcare services in Italy can be costly for non-residents. It should cover hospital stays, emergency treatments, and repatriation if necessary.
- **Trip Interruption and Cancellation:** This coverage helps if you need to cancel or cut short your trip due to unforeseen circumstances like illness or family emergencies.

- **Theft and Loss:** Look for insurance that covers stolen or lost items, including luggage, electronics, and personal belongings.

Tip: Keep a copy of your travel insurance policy and emergency contact information easily accessible during your trip. Many insurers also offer 24/7 assistance hotlines.

5. What to Do in an Emergency

In the unlikely event that you find yourself in an emergency situation, here's a quick step-by-step guide:

1. Stay Calm and Assess the Situation: Take a moment to breathe and evaluate what's happening. This will help you make clearer decisions.
2. Call the Appropriate Emergency Number: Depending on your situation, dial 112 for general emergencies, 118 for medical help, or 112 for police assistance.
3. Provide Clear Information: When speaking to emergency operators, give them your location (address or nearby landmark) and describe the situation as clearly as possible. Many operators speak English, but knowing a few basic Italian phrases can be helpful (e.g., "Aiuto!" means "Help!").
4. Follow Instructions: Stay on the line and follow any instructions the emergency operator

gives you. If you're in a public place, look for nearby locals or staff who may be able to assist.

B. Health and Wellness

1. Finding Pharmacies (Farmacie) in Northern Italy

Pharmacies in Italy are called farmacie, and they are easy to spot with their green cross sign. They are your go-to for over-the-counter medications, basic medical supplies, and health advice. Pharmacists in Italy are highly trained and can often help with minor ailments like colds, allergies, and upset stomachs.

- **What to Expect:** Most pharmacies are open from 8:30 AM to 12:30 PM and 3:30 PM to 7:30 PM, Monday to Saturday. However, many cities have 24-hour pharmacies (farmacie di turno) that are open after hours for emergencies.
- **How to Find One:** Look for the green cross sign or use Google Maps to search for "farmacia" nearby. Many hotels and tourist information centers can also direct you to the nearest pharmacy.

Tip: If you need medication outside regular hours, check the notice board outside any pharmacy. It usually lists the address of the nearest open farmacia di turno.

Popular Pharmacy Chains:
- **Lloyds Farmacia:** Known for its wide selection and helpful staff.
- **Farmacia Comunale:** Often found in city centers and offers 24-hour services in larger cities like Milan and Venice.

2. Over-the-Counter Medications in Italy

Italian pharmacies carry a variety of over-the-counter medications, but keep in mind that brand names may differ from what you're used to. Here are some common equivalents:

- **For Pain Relief:** If you're looking for something like Tylenol or Advil, ask for Paracetamolo (similar to acetaminophen) or Ibuprofene (ibuprofen).
- **For Colds or Allergies:** Look for medications labeled Antistaminico for allergies (similar to Claritin) or Decongestionante for nasal congestion.
- **For Stomach Issues:** If you need something for an upset stomach, ask for Plasil (for nausea) or Gaviscon (for heartburn and indigestion).

Tip: Pharmacists often speak English, especially in tourist areas, but it's helpful to know the Italian names for common medications. Don't hesitate to ask for advice—they're very knowledgeable and can recommend the best option.

3. Medical Assistance and Hospitals

In case of a more serious health issue, you may need to visit a hospital or urgent care clinic. Italy has a high-quality healthcare system, and many hospitals in Northern Italy offer English-speaking services, especially in major cities and tourist areas.

- **Emergency Medical Assistance:** For immediate medical help, dial 118, the emergency number for ambulance services. This number is free and works throughout Italy.
- **Hospital Care:** Most hospitals (ospedali) have an emergency room (Pronto Soccorso) that handles urgent medical needs. Be prepared for a wait, as emergency rooms prioritize patients based on the severity of their condition.
- **Urgent Care Clinics:** If your issue isn't life-threatening but still needs prompt attention, consider visiting an urgent care clinic (Guardia Medica). These clinics are usually open after regular hours and can handle minor injuries, illnesses, and prescriptions.

Top Hospitals in Northern Italy:

Ospedale Niguarda (Milan): One of the largest hospitals in Italy, offering comprehensive medical services and English-speaking staff.
- **Contact**: +39 02 64441
- **Address**: Piazza dell'Ospedale Maggiore 3, 20162 Milan, Italy

Ospedale Civile di Venezia (Venice): Known for its high-quality care and convenient location near the city center.
- **Contact**: +39 041 529 4111
- **Address**: Campo Santi Giovanni e Paolo 636, 30122 Venice, Italy

4. Travel Health Insurance

Having travel health insurance is highly recommended when visiting Italy, as it can cover unexpected medical costs, including doctor visits, hospital stays, and medication.

- **What It Covers:** Travel health insurance typically covers emergency medical treatment, prescription medications, and emergency evacuation if necessary. It's a safety net that can save you a lot of stress and money if something goes wrong.
- **How to Use It:** If you need medical assistance, keep a copy of your insurance policy and emergency contact number with you. Many hospitals will treat you and bill your insurance directly, but you may need to pay upfront for minor services and submit a claim later.

Tip: Check with your insurance provider before your trip to understand what's covered and get a list of in-network providers in Italy.

C. Language Tips and Useful Italian Phrases

1. Basic Greetings and Polite Expressions

Knowing how to greet people and use polite expressions is a great start. These simple phrases will help you make a good first impression.

- **Hello / Hi:** Ciao (chow)
- **Good morning / Good day:** Buongiorno (bwohn-jor-noh)
- **Good evening:** Buonasera (bwohn-ah-seh-rah)
- **Goodbye:** Arrivederci (ah-ree-veh-der-chee)
- **Please:** Per favore (pehr fah-voh-reh)
- **Thank you:** Grazie (graht-see-eh)
- **You're welcome:** Prego (preh-goh)
- **Excuse me / Sorry:** Mi scusi (mee skoo-zee)
- **Yes:** Sì (see)
- **No:** No (noh)

Tip: Italians tend to be friendly and expressive. Adding a smile while saying "grazie" or "buongiorno" will make your interaction even warmer.

2. Getting Around: Directions and Transportation

These phrases will be helpful when you're navigating cities, asking for directions, or using public transportation.

Where is...?: Dov'è...? (doh-veh)
- **Example**: **Dov'è la stazione?** (Where is the train station?)

How much is a ticket to Milan?: Quanto costa un biglietto per Milano? (kwahn-toh koh-stah oon bee-lyet-toh pehr mee-lah-noh)

I would like a ticket, please: Vorrei un biglietto, per favore. (voh-ray oon bee-lyet-toh pehr fah-voh-reh)

Where is the nearest bus stop?: Dov'è la fermata dell'autobus più vicina? (doh-veh lah fehr-mah-tah dell ow-toh-boos pyoo vee-chee-nah)

Left / Right / Straight ahead: Sinistra (see-nee-strah) / Destra (deh-strah) / Dritto (dreet-toh)

Tip: Use Google Maps for navigation, but don't be afraid to ask a local for directions—they'll often give you great tips and shortcuts.

3. Ordering Food and Drinks

Italian cuisine is a highlight of any trip to Northern Italy, and knowing how to order your food and drinks in Italian makes the experience even better.

I would like…: Vorrei… (voh-ray)
   Example: Vorrei un cappuccino. (I would like a cappuccino.)
Can I have the menu, please?: Posso avere il menu, per favore? (pohs-soh ah-veh-reh eel meh-noo pehr fah-voh-reh)
The check, please: Il conto, per favore. (eel kohn-toh pehr fah-voh-reh)
Delicious!: Delizioso! (deh-lee-tsee-oh-zoh)
What do you recommend?: Cosa mi consiglia? (koh-zah mee kohn-seel-yah)
Water (still / sparkling): Acqua (naturale / frizzante) (ahk-kwah nah-too-rah-leh / freet-tsahn-teh)

Tip: Italians love their coffee, but be mindful of when you order certain types. Cappuccino is usually only ordered in the morning, while an espresso (un caffè) is preferred after meals.

4. Shopping and Payments

If you're exploring local markets, boutique shops, or picking up souvenirs, these phrases will come in handy.

How much does this cost?: Quanto costa? (kwahn-toh koh-stah)

I'll take it: Lo prendo. (loh prehn-doh)
Do you accept credit cards?: Accettate carte di credito? (ah-cheht-tah-teh kar-teh dee kreh-dee-toh)
Can I have a receipt, please?: Posso avere la ricevuta, per favore? (pohs-soh ah-veh-reh lah ree-cheh-voo-tah pehr fah-voh-reh)
Is there a discount?: C'è uno sconto? (cheh oo-noh skohn-toh)

Tip: In Italy, many small shops and markets prefer cash, especially for smaller purchases. It's good to carry some euros with you.

5. Emergency Phrases

In case of an emergency, these phrases can be crucial.

Help!: Aiuto! (ah-yoo-toh)
I need a doctor: Ho bisogno di un medico. (oh bee-zoh-nyoh dee oon meh-dee-koh)
Call an ambulance!: Chiami un'ambulanza! (kee-ah-mee oon ahm-boo-lahn-tsah)
I've lost my passport: Ho perso il mio passaporto. (oh pehr-soh eel mee-oh pahs-sah-por-toh)
Where is the nearest pharmacy?: Dov'è la farmacia più vicina? (doh-veh lah fahr-mah-chee-ah pyoo vee-chee-nah)

Tip: If you're unsure how to explain something in Italian, it's okay to ask, "Parla inglese?" (Do you speak English?). Many people in tourist areas will know at least a little English.

Conclusion

Congratulations on choosing the Northern Italy Travel Guide 2025! We're thrilled you picked this book to accompany you on your journey through one of the world's most captivating regions. Northern Italy is a place of enchanting beauty, rich history, and vibrant culture, and we hope this guide has made your adventure even more delightful and unforgettable.

Within these pages, we've explored Northern Italy's iconic cities—from the fashion capital of Milan to the romantic canals of Venice, and from the Renaissance splendor of Florence to the charming towns of Verona and Turin. Each city holds its own unique treasures, and we hope our insights have helped you uncover them in ways that resonate with your soul.

This guide has led you through Northern Italy's diverse landscapes, from the serene beauty of the Italian Lakes to the majestic peaks of the Dolomites, and from the colorful villages of Cinque Terre to the rolling hills of Tuscany. We hope you've enjoyed immersing yourself in these breathtaking sights and creating memories that will last a lifetime.

But Northern Italy is more than just scenery and cities. It's a place where history, art, and culture intertwine. From ancient Roman ruins to

Renaissance masterpieces, and from traditional festivals to the warmth of the Italian people, we hope you've experienced the true essence of this captivating region.

We've also provided practical tips to enhance your travels, from navigating transportation to savoring authentic cuisine. Whether you chose to indulge in fine dining, explore local markets, or sip on exquisite wines, we hope our suggestions have helped you appreciate the true flavors of Northern Italy.

As you depart, we hope you carry with you the memories of charming piazzas, breathtaking vistas, and the warmth of Italian hospitality. Northern Italy is more than just a destination—it's an experience that awakens the senses and leaves a lasting impression on the heart.

Thank you for letting the Northern Italy Travel Guide 2025 be your companion on this adventure. May the spirit of Italy stay with you, and may your travels continue to inspire and enrich your life. Safe travels, and we hope to see you back in Northern Italy soon!

Warm regards,

The Northern Italy Travel Guide 2025 Team

Bonus: Authentic Northern Italian Recipes

As a special bonus, we're delighted to share some of Northern Italy's most beloved traditional recipes. Each dish reflects the rich culinary heritage and diverse regional flavors of this captivating region, from handmade pasta and creamy risotto to hearty stews and decadent desserts. These recipes capture the essence of Northern Italian cuisine—simple, fresh, and bursting with flavor.

1. Risotto alla Milanese (Saffron Risotto)

This iconic Milanese dish is a creamy, flavorful risotto infused with the golden hue and delicate aroma of saffron. It's a classic comfort food that's perfect for any occasion.

1. Risotto alla Milanese (Saffron Risotto)

This creamy rice dish is a classic of Milanese cuisine, known for its vibrant yellow color and delicate saffron flavor.

Ingredients:

- 1.5 liters chicken or vegetable broth
- 1 onion, finely chopped
- 2 tablespoons butter
- 1 cup Arborio rice

- 1/2 cup dry white wine
- 1 pinch saffron threads
- 1/2 cup grated Parmesan cheese
- Salt and pepper to taste

Instructions:

1. In a saucepan, heat the broth to a simmer.
2. In a separate pot, melt the butter over medium heat. Add the onion and cook until softened.
3. Add the rice and stir until toasted. Pour in the wine and cook until absorbed.
4. Add a ladleful of hot broth to the rice and stir until absorbed. Continue adding broth, one ladleful at a time, stirring constantly, until the rice is cooked through but still al dente (about 20 minutes).
5. Stir in the saffron threads and Parmesan cheese. Season with salt and pepper.
6. Serve immediately, garnished with extra Parmesan cheese if desired.

2. Osso Buco (Braised Veal Shanks)

This hearty Milanese specialty features tender veal shanks braised in white wine, vegetables, and broth until they're fall-off-the-bone delicious. It's a true celebration of Northern Italian comfort food.

Ingredients:

- 4 veal shanks
- 1/4 cup all-purpose flour
- 2 tablespoons olive oil
- 1 onion, chopped
- 2 carrots, chopped
- 2 celery stalks, chopped
- 1 cup dry white wine
- 1 cup beef broth
- 1 bay leaf
- Grated zest of 1 lemon
- Salt and pepper to taste
- Gremolata (see recipe below) for garnish

Instructions:

1. Preheat oven to 325°F (160°C). Season the veal shanks with salt and pepper and dredge in flour.
2. Heat olive oil in a large Dutch oven over medium-high heat. Brown the veal shanks on all sides.
3. Remove the shanks and add the onion, carrots, and celery to the pot. Cook until softened.
4. Add the wine and cook until reduced by half.
5. Return the veal shanks to the pot. Add the broth, bay leaf, and lemon zest. Bring to a simmer.
6. Cover and transfer to the oven. Braise for 2-2.5 hours, or until the meat is very tender.
7. Serve hot, garnished with gremolata.

Gremolata:

- 1/4 cup chopped fresh parsley

- 2 cloves garlic, minced
- 1 tablespoon grated lemon zest

3. Pesto alla Genovese (Basil Pesto)

This vibrant green sauce is a staple of Ligurian cuisine, originating in Genoa. Made with fresh basil, pine nuts, garlic, Parmesan cheese, and olive oil, it's a versatile condiment that's perfect for pasta, sandwiches, and more.

Ingredients:

- 2 cups fresh basil leaves
- 1/4 cup pine nuts
- 2 cloves garlic
- 1/2 cup grated Parmesan cheese
- 1/2 cup extra virgin olive oil
- Salt and pepper to taste

Instructions:

1. In a food processor, combine the basil, pine nuts, garlic, and Parmesan cheese. Pulse until finely chopped.
2. With the motor running, slowly drizzle in the olive oil until a smooth paste forms.
3. Season with salt and pepper.
4. Use immediately or store in an airtight container in the refrigerator for up to a week.

4. Tiramisu

This classic Italian dessert is a decadent treat featuring layers of coffee-soaked ladyfingers, creamy mascarpone filling, and cocoa powder. It's a perfect ending to any Italian meal.

Ingredients:

- 1 cup strong brewed coffee, cooled
- 1/4 cup coffee liqueur (optional)
- 24 ladyfingers
- 1 cup mascarpone cheese
- 1/2 cup heavy cream
- 1/4 cup sugar
- 2 egg yolks
- Cocoa powder for dusting

Instructions:

1. In a shallow dish, combine the coffee and coffee liqueur (if using).
2. Dip each ladyfinger into the coffee mixture, turning quickly to coat both sides.
3. Arrange half of the ladyfingers in the bottom of a 8x8 inch baking dish.
4. In a bowl, beat the mascarpone cheese, heavy cream, sugar, and egg yolks until smooth and creamy.
5. Spread half of the mascarpone mixture over the ladyfingers.
6. Repeat layers with remaining ladyfingers and mascarpone mixture.

7. Dust the top with cocoa powder.
8. Refrigerate for at least 4 hours before serving.

Buon appetito!

Made in the USA
Middletown, DE
21 February 2025

71625424R00118